ELEMENTAL FENG SHUI

THE ART OF ORIENTATION

M. CHARLYNE CHIASSON, B.I.D., D.F.S

TESTIMONIALS

In our hunger and search for more knowledge, Charlyne and I often met all over the world as co-students over many years, studying with great teachers: Prof. Dr. Jes Lim and Eric Dowsett. I was immediately taken by her creativity and her inspirational way of discussing the things we learned. And now she has put it in writing!

This book can serve many. It is an excellent reference guide for those new to the subject. It is also excellent for those of you who are more advanced and professional in the field to refresh your knowledge and a book you can give to your clients for them to better understand Feng Shui. It is also a great introduction for all those in the design and development fields.

A delight to read, it gives a simple yet deep overview of what Feng Shui is about. It is clear that Charlyne has a profound knowledge of Feng Shui and the Elements: that's the reason why she can write about it in such a succinct yet engaging way without getting into too many details that make other books on the subject so confusing!

—*Jinny Thielsch, Astrologer, Feng Shui Consultant and Tao Geomantic Master in the Netherlands*

After moving into our new house we had the daunting task of making it more livable. We were situated opposite a t-junction and the yard was completely exposed to the public. Cars coming down on the road opposite our living room could see into our house and yard. We needed some privacy! Also, the property is thin and long, sloping down towards the back. We had an earthen berm built along the front of the land, then approached Charlyne to help us with improvements since the layout still didn't feel right.

She evaluated us, our property and our needs. She was able to explain why it didn't 'feel right'. She knew where the energy wasn't moving and where energy was just 'rushing out' or escaping. I liked that she didn't tell me exactly what I should do, but allowed me to come up with my own solutions. Armed with the knowledge I had gained from Charlyne, I was able to decide where to put up fences to create outdoor rooms, where to put my office inside the building and so on.

The results were amazing. We really love living here now. Our house feels cozy, but not too tight. Our indoor and outdoor spaces flow beautifully together and we are always gently encouraged to be outdoors as much as indoors.

Working with Charlyne was pleasant and she really cares, since she followed up to check on the actions we took. Naturally, I can recommend her highly, since working with a professional of higher pedigree alway pays off. We put our business in the 'business corner' of the building, and learned to keep the 'relationship corner' always activated. It was and still is an overall wonderful experience.

—*Heribert Eisinger, Designer, Builder and owner of Cowichan Fine Interiors*

Charlyne came to my property several times and coached me over a period of a year, to create something beautiful on the land. She came to dowse for underground water and energy spots, helping me to find out where my buildings should go. Charlyne also created the whole design of my cabin. Her support was always comprehensive, including her knowledge of Feng Shui and interior design as well as being able to shift energies practically during the whole process. She has a lovely and empowering way and therefore I can really recommend her and the wisdon in this book.

—*Anita Wyssmann Smith, Switerland & Slocan Valley BC , Canada*

Charlyne was my roommate periodically from 2013-2015 while doing contracts in Calgary. She loved my home there as it had a great view of the city. She shared with me the importance of good Ming Tang. Years later, newly single, I moved to Vancouver. I was embarking on a massive life shift and a new career in film. I felt lucky to find an apartment within my budget. The huge shift from sunny Calgary to the gloomy coastal climate did not help when I was waiting for the calls to happen and for money to flow.

When Charlyne would visit she would say, "you really need an apartment on the other side of the building, the one with the great Ming Tang!" Unexpectedly, I had water damage in my apartment and I asked if I could move to a newly vacated unit, one with the incredible mountain, city and ocean views. What a difference it made! It was clean with light bouncing everywhere making it abundant with energy and hope.

Charlyne was so right, the shift to a great Ming Tang changed my life. In no time at all everything happened. Job calls started to pour in, money appeared, and best of all, my well being and energy were restored. My relationships also became balanced. Such an amazing experience thanks to understanding the power of a good Ming Tang!

—*Amelia Montserrat Cabezón Sanchez, Vancouver BC Canada*

Charlyne is a creative, intuitive, and resourceful practitioner who has assited me with many projects over the past 15 years. From transforming a basement apartment into an energetic, funky oasis, to creating 'office tour' worthy spaces in stogy government offices. In each case the benefits were tangible. When I acquired a 130 yr. old home she energetically cleared it inside an out. Then, with her Design and Feng Shui expertise, she assited me with activating the entrance, with room selection, bed placement, colour choices and furniture layouts right down to the plants' locations that would best activate spaces. In the yard and garden she sugggested changes to pedestrian traffic patterns with the placement of gateways, fences, planters, fire pits etc. The result was a calm yet vibrant sanctuary. For more than ten years I have recommended Charlyne's coaching to many who have felt that their environments were 'just not right'. They, too, have benefitted from her insight, energetic personal coaching and recommendations.

The gift of this book is her sharing the Feng Shui experience. I have no doubt it can bring you the tangible benefits of abundance, peace, and flow in your 'home and offices' spaces.

—*Monica Kendel, Homeowner/ landlord, Executive Coach, Victoria, BC*

Few have the attuning skills and awareness to translate the ancient wisdom of nature, landscape and the art of design as beautifully as Charlyne. She is a gifted diviner who possesses extraordinary knowledge of the elements and their essence within Feng Shui. In this ground-breaking book she shares vital information as both a reference guide and for practical application in our homes and our lives. An essential tool in every library.

—*Ashala Yardley, Cultural Anthropologist, Author, Educator, Vancouver, BC*

TABLE OF CONTENTS

SECTION THREE:
Feng Shui Application: Space by Space   **95**

NOTABLE ILLUSTRATIONS, CHARTS and ANECDOTES

DEDICATION

For clean Air and Water on the Planet

Feng and Shui

To All Seekers of Truth and Wonderment

and the memory of

Moses Daniel Chiasson

who inspired exactly that in me

"There is no logical way to discover of these elemental laws. There is only the way of Intuition, which is helped by a feeling for the order lying behind appearance." **Albert Einstein**

Architecture
Gas and Oil
Chefs/Cooking
Movie Production
Visual Arts
Costume and Clothing Design
Photography

Fire

Builders/ Landscapers
Farmers/ Livestock
Mining
Real Estate/ Construction
Reycycling
Environmentalist
Warehousing

Earth

Developers
Investors/ Traders
Mechanics
Computer Hardware
Surgeons
Engineers
Transportation

Metal

Designers
Medicine &
Researchers
Personnel
Fishing
Firefighters
Importers /Exporters

Water

Decorators
Astrology
Animation
Spiritually Expansive Careers
Paper Products
Woodworkers
Inventors

Wood

The Elements and Who We Are
Personally and Professionally

As humans, we embody all elements, but did you know you choose your work based on specific elemental combinations present at the time of your birth? The elements Fire, Earth, Metal, Water and Wood in various combinations mold our individual personalities and often many of the choices we make.

In exploring this theory I hope to reveal the impulse behind what you are drawn to do for your livelihood. Success and the intuitive process go hand and hand. Exploring these insights may allow a deeper understanding of your personal process, environment and how to maximize being in the flow.

It is imperative to share Feng Shui knowledge with architectural, design, decor, building and development related professions. The goal is to create better, more informed ecologically based design. As we face intense global shifts it is important to know there are simple solutions that can be co-creative with nature.

FIRE

Do you have a profession or a longing to be creative in a way that inspires and evokes responses? Does what you do, allow others to see your creations? Do you evoke passion and vision for others to follow? A yes to these questions would put you into the Fire professions: architects, artists, photographers, clothing designers, chefs, costume and creative makeup artists, actors, etc.

EARTH

Do you work with the land? Do you cultivate the earth? Is what you do ultimately nourishing for those around you? Do you take care of things? Are you the invisible force behind what gets done? A yes to these inquiries would see you in an Earth profession. Earth people are builders, gardeners, massage therapist, systems analysts, nurses, etc.

METAL

Does your work demand precision and control? Have you the ability to look at challenges from various angles? Can you organize and lead a team? A yes to these questions would see you as someone who embodies Metal. Metal people are developers, tool and dye designers, astronauts, surgeons, team captains, department heads, etc.

Fishing in the Indian Ocean; an age old connection to Water.

1) Firey energy fuels this soapstone sculptures work.

2) Carpenters and Builders manipulate Wood to create beauty.

WATER

Do you work in a way that requires deep concentration? Do you contemplate to find answers to questions, challenges and problems? Does your mode of working involve solitude, quiet and insight? Are you an adventurer and naturally curious? Affirmative response may find you resonate with Water. These deep thinkers are designers, human resource people, private consultants, teachers, transportation specialists, medical research, or work in the fishing industry, tourism, avalanche safety, etc.

WOOD

Do you have creative and dynamic ideas? Are you able to inspire people with solutions to tough problems? Can you inspire a team with positive outgoing energy? Is your energy hard to contain? A yes to these questions means you emulate Wood. Illustration, decorating, real estate, planning, forestry, animation, creative development businesses and natural food production are professions associated with Wood.

When you are able to understand your personal impulses you can then best choose a profession that suits you. Knowing the professions that feed your energy and element can broaden your perspective, define your choices and create greater harmony in your career path. Also knowing how to activate the areas in your home that support your elements and career can bring positive change.

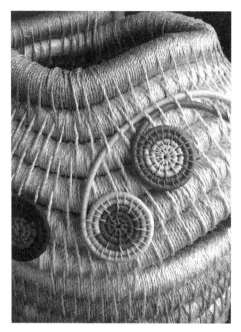

3) This hand crafted piece shows all the elements. Fire in its creative inception and vision. Earth in the colours. Water in the the flow and curves. Metal in the round and spiral shapes and Wood in the materials used. Fire is however the basic impulse in a profession that creates, inspires and evokes response from the viewer.

4) Elementical Chi is magnified within the scale of this awe inspiring architecture.

INTRODUCTION :

That's so Feng Shui!

What's up with the Feng Shui?

The Feng Shui is so wrong!

*Have these phrases
passed your way lately?*

The term Feng Shui has been bandied about in the design world for years now. Some take it seriously and others dismiss it. Anyone can profess to have Feng Shui knowledge. Twenty-five years ago there were few books written but today there are thousands. As a profession it is not regulated, and barely understood.

There are few aware of the different schools of Feng Shui and the many ways of practicing this ancient art in the modern world.

Feng Shui is having an impact on building world wide. More noticeable in Asian cities like Hong Kong and Singapore, architecture is clearly being influenced by its ideologies. When we look deeper we find many threads of basic wisdom in its practices and how many cultures use the ideologies without giving it a name.

The intention, which lay at the core of Feng Shui, is to understand how its practice aligns to basic human nature and how its concepts actually cross cultures worldwide.

5) Colonial Architecture creates a rounded corner which softens the edge, directs flow and is in effect good Feng Shui.

6) Animism, Hinduism and Buddhism are the combined spiritual practices in Bali, Indonesia. Here a traditional temple is decorated for Chinese New Year.

This light infused space in a medical facility creates hope and expansion.

7) Living design that combines innovation, the elements and Feng Shui in a unique way.

Feng Shui / Wind Water that is tranquil and serene.

8) Tropical architecture creating flow.

Getting Elemental

In 2009 I had the privilege of designing a Feng Shui home for a client with Asian ancestry. I was thrilled at the possibilities of doing such a project as I had never before designed a Feng Shui building. Clear objectives start with a good facility program which involves gathering a myriad of information. This is then assimilated into a predesign. Considerations like location, setting, direction, weather and adjacent structures are essential for proper design and crucial for Feng Shui investigation and application. Landing a facility programmer position right after design school taught me to use all my investigative skills and be thorough. My Feng Shui design ideas had to fit the site, style, needs, and budget of the client and be easily conveyed to the architect.

It was during this project that I realized that relating Feng Shui concepts was not easy. Although I did submit full architectural design drawings encompassing Feng Shui Design concepts the translation was flawed and ideas were unfortunately misunderstood.

Clearly a new format was needed to explain Feng Shui principles to the design profession and for all those interested in the concepts and use of Feng Shui. The goal is to share this knowledge by emphasizing practical design and how this ancient wisdom can make the ordinary, extraordinary.

The core of Feng Shui knowledge is the understanding and application of the five elements. Known as the Five Transformations this theory is at the core of all Asian modalities, such as Qi Gong, Tai Chi, Feng Shui, Tao/Zen gardens, Traditional Chinese medicine and Tibetan healing practices. What we choose as a livelihood is often based on our personal elemental energy. Knowing which of the five elements we represent and how we embody them deepens both our personal and world view. All professions or livelihoods have an interactive relationship within the Five transformations. Its understanding illustrates our strengths and weaknesses. We learn how best to cooperate with others to maximize our talents. Feng Shui and elemental wisdom can create sustainable, energized spaces in which to thrive.

9) Wind=Feng and Water=Shui; it is the core of our being and our landscapes, creating clouds and tides.

What is Feng Shui really?

A common answer is that Feng Shui is an ancient art of placement. To many this equates to a home's placement on land and how the furnishings are placed within it. While both are true, this interpretation limits the broadness of its deeper application and understanding. Although the words are Chinese, the concept is universal. The literal translation of Feng is Wind and Shui being Water. If we break down these terms conceptually, wind becomes the oxygen we breathe or the cosmic breath of life which arrives at birth and leaves us at death; Feng=Wind=Breath. Shui translates as water, of which we are primarily composed; Shui=Water=Life. Without breath or water we perish. Seven years into my study, I discovered the need to broaden my application and understanding of Feng Shui beyond being strictly a design aid. I recognized that these basic concepts exist in every culture in the world. We are human, we are living and breathing Wind/Water. Understanding this at a deeper level, allowed my relationship to my craft to evolve. I became a translator of an ancient art made popular through Chinese culture. This gave me a platform to practice and teach a much larger concept.

What is known as Feng Shui today has been translated cross culturally for over 1000 years but has just started to make its presence felt in Western Culture. This foreign concept and its limited tenure has met with raised eyebrows. In practicing and learning this craft for over 24 years I feel compelled to impart the core of what Feng Shui is, as seen through the eyes of a Feng Shui designer/consultant/geomancer.

As the world continues to shrink we can only benefit from having simple references to what is valued in other cultures as good design. Although old, this view of 'human placement' can refresh our practices and add to what we know. I invite you to join me through a practical and informed examination of the essence of Feng Shui as applied to Architecture, Building, Development, Interior Design and Decorating. I also invite people from all occupations to discover your basic elemental nature, so you too can apply it to your life and profession.

Becoming Personally Activated

My first session with Dr. Jess Lim, who would become my long standing Feng shui master, was in San Fransisco in 2001. I had studied and practised Feng Shui for 7 years at this point, so it was an awakening to hear his explanation. Urging the class to take a deep breath he referred to it as the 'cosmic breath of life' or wind the meaning of Feng. Then he asked 'what percentage the body was made up of water.' It then registered that I was it, that Feng Shui was me, not just some mystical, superstitious Asian practice, but how we place the human body on the planet, for the best health and well-being possible. This revelation radically shifted my perspective. It gave me a unique view point from which to share the discipline to which I was so drawn. During that first meeting with Master Lim he energetically 'activated' a deeper desire to understand this work. Almost immediately my life started to open in mystical and magical ways. I have not looked back.

TERMS AND CONCEPTS

There are many new ideas to embrace when exploring Feng Shui. This list of extensive terms, definitions and concepts along with various illustrations will better convey their meanings. This extensive list is not in alphabetical order but laid out for step by step understanding of Feng Shui concepts. **For ease of reference these are listed alphabetically as highlighted terms in the index.**

Feng : Means wind; the cosmic breath of life as our breath.
Concept : Wind or Feng is considered destructive without the presence of Water in Feng Shui.

Shui : Means water; which makes up over 85% of the human body.
Concept : In Feng Shui practice it equates with life force energy and abundance. Observe how and where it flows and what happens when it is blocked or diverted. Water as metaphor for flow in life; is the flow easy or difficult? In the landscape it is referred to as the Dragons Veins or waterways that cut through the land and mountain sides. It is essential for all life forms to exist.

Feng Shui : Literally, Wind / Water; their interaction in nature and how the human body interacts within its environment.
Concept : An optimal combination of wind and water creates a balance of energy distribution. It is this ancient art of placement which allows us to either find or create optimum locations for human interaction, building sites, homes, monuments and gardens. Originally used in China for grave placement, its use was expanded and modified during the early dynasties to enable and empower the emperors and their courts.

Chi : The Chinese word for energy.
Concept : Chi refers to the vital life force energy as reflected in many cultures. In Japan there are over 900 words in the language which contain the word or prefix Ki/Chi. In Feng Shui, water, money and abundance are metaphors for Chi and Energy. Investigating levels and locations of optimal Chi is of primary importance in Feng Shui.

Yin & Yang : The two contrasting and opposing qualities of Chi or energy.

Yang : Is the light, outgoing and visible quality of energy. It aligns with masculine energy, sunrise, springtime and brightness, sweet and outgoing.

Yin : is the dark, subversive, and the hidden quality of energy. It aligns with the feminine, dark, midnight, winter, bitter and hidden energies.
Concept : Yang is the balance and opposite of Yin, and as such they form an opposing yet dynamic balance to each other when in equal flow. When one or the other is dominant this often indicates imbalance or dynamic shift.

10) Illustration by MCC

In interior spaces it appears visually when there is an overuse of the same materials and colors.

There needs to be contrast to have balance. Yin and Yang go beyond the physical and is often felt in a space or a piece of land that has anomalies that are metaphysical, geophysical or electromagnetic nature. Examples: An unmarked burial site may feel uncomfortable, whether you are aware that you are on or near one. Yin energy, metaphysical in nature, is in a higher concentration creating an imbalance. High Yang energy may be experienced by way of fast flowing underground water, which is geophysical in nature.

Five Transformations : Also known as the 5 Elements, the Five Transformations refer to the dynamic interaction between Fire, Earth, Metal, Water and Wood.
Concept : The five element theory is the basic tenet of all the Asian healing arts. Its study is crucial in understanding how chi flows in Feng Shui, Traditional Chinese & Tibetan Medicine, Qi Gung and Tai Chi. Covered in depth in Section Two, the Five Transformations is an integrated system that can take years to master yet it's basic in Feng Shui Design. Balancing the elements is done by the use of symbology, color, texture and placement. The five elements have a unique interdependence within the professions of Architecture, Building, Development, Design and Decoration.

Bagua or Pa Qua : The Bagua is an octagon shaped tool used in Feng Shui as an energy compass. It places an important aspect of life into each of its eight sections that are aligned with each compass direction. In Asia a more traditional, complex tool called the Lopan is used by Feng Shui practitioners and masters. The Bagua is a much simpler form of the Lopan. It conveys information in a way that is easier for Western users. Each compass direction is referred to as a Gua, thus a collection of Guas is referred to as Bagua or Pa Qua in some publications.
Concept : Each Gua of the Bagua represents an essential, basic principle. This information is aligned to directions, elements, numbers and the Trigrams of the I Ching. These Trigrams are a symbolic arrangement of three solid and three broken lines. They represent the principles of Thunder, Wind, Fire, Earth, Lake, Heaven, Water and Mountain. In Feng Shui these translate into various universal concepts. Wind is Fortunate Blessings; Fire is Vision and Fame; Earth is Relationship; Lake is Creativity and Children; Heaven is Helpful People, Travel; Water is Career and Mountain is Knowledge. Although eight sided, the center contains a portion of each of the eight energies and is referred to as the Tai Chi or Sacred Center. The Bagua, when used on a floor plan is transposed from a compass style octagon to a 9 sectioned square with each being the same size or 1/9th of a square. This shape is easily placed over a piece of land, building or microsited into a room to locate the various energies or principles.

Magic Square : There are many types of magic squares but in Feng Shui it is a square divided into nine separate sections. The layout of numbers will always add up to the same sum, no matter how you add them: up, down, across or diagonally.

Concept : The Magic Square coincides with how the numbers are found on the Bagua or Feng Shui compass. The layout of the numbers in the Feng Shui Magic Square forms the Nine Star Ki Path. The numbers and their relationship to the elements is the basis for Nine Star Ki Astrology which is used in Feng Shui. The use of nine numbers is also the basis of many numerological systems world wide.

Nine Star Ki Astrology : Called Feng Shui astrology, Nine Star Ki examines an individual's personality based on the five elements. Each element and number has characteristics that affect health, relationships, career choices and personality.

Concept : Unlike Western astrology this system deals with only the 7 stars of the Big Dipper with a Yin star (Vega) and Yang star (Polaris) These nine stars are represented by an element, a direction and a number. We each have a set of personal stars that are determined by our birth year, date and month. There are three numbers that make up our personal combination. They are known as the Principle

Star (basic adult personality) the Character Star (our childhood personality and the root of our emotional body) and the Energetic Star (how we appear to others). It is an effective way to determine both personality traits and tendencies. It is used as a guide for career, relationship and timing of projects. Each number aligns with a specific location on the Bagua.

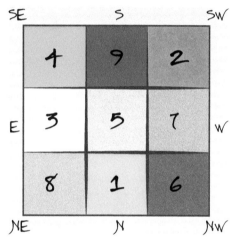

The Magic Square

The Simple Bagua Compass: With Eight Directions or Guas and Center

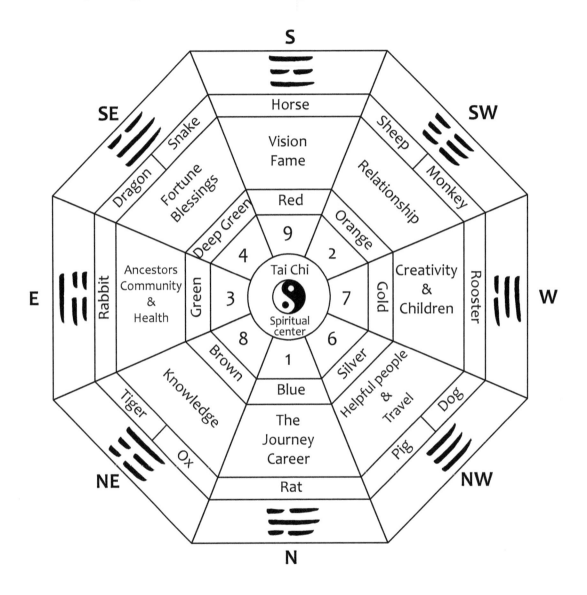

BAGUA: A simple Feng Shui compass shows the location of animals of the Chinese horoscope, universal energies, trigrams of the I Ching, directions, colors, and magic square or Nine Star Ki numbers.

THE ELEMENTS & PERSONALITY: Nine Star Ki Astrology

In Nine Star Ki Astrology the numbers are dictated by the seven stars of the constellation Ursus Major (The Big Dipper) and two additional stars Polaris and Vega. These two stars serve as the Yin and Yang stars which balance the constellation as it moves through the sky with the seasons. This group of nine stars is the basis of the Nine Star Ki Astrological system used in Feng Shui. Each number is aligned with an element and a direction rendering each unique.

Nine Star Ki Astrology

Used as a tool for personal guidance, it is also valuable for Feng Shui Analysis.

Nine Star Ki is paramount for understanding the 5 elemental transformations and how they affect us on individual levels. Each section of the Bagua or Feng Shui Compass has an element, a number and specific energy.

Fire is located in the South and Water in the North. As the two most powerful and dynamic elements they get one direction each. Earth has three locations on the Bagua; NE, SW and the Center, also known as the Tai Chi. Wood and Metal have two locations each. Wood is located in the East and SE and Metal occupies the West and NW. The 5 elements are aligned with 9 personality types. Of the various types of Chinese astrology used in Feng Shui, Nine Star Ki is a simple and effective way to understand clients and their personalities. It reveals information about character traits, career choices, relationships and health issues.

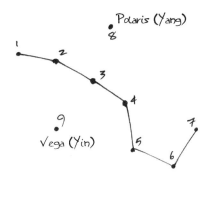

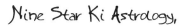

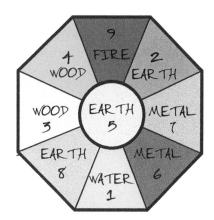

Bagua with Numbers of the Nine Star Ki System

The constellation shows the stars numbered and the location of Polaris and Vega. The direction/location on the Bagua compass that each number lives is referred to as its house. The joining of the numbers from one to nine shows the Nine Star Ki Path within the Magic Square. Each number moves from house to house on a daily, monthly, annually and twenty year cycle. In depth study of Nine Star Ki can be a life long pursuit in itself. Polaris, currently the North Star, is believed to change places with Vega every 165,000 years. Note that this time frame changes depending on what publication is referenced.

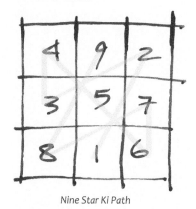

Nine Star Ki Path

Nine Star Path : When a line is drawn from one to nine it forms a pattern known as the Nine Star Ki Path. This is aligned to Saturn and sacred geometry.

Concept : The Nine Star Path charts one's Principle Number as it moves through each house determined by the daily, monthly, annual and 20 year cycles. As one's number moves through the houses different influences are experienced. The Nine Star Ki path is useful for timing and planning of events. For example; A # 1 Water person may feel less comfortable in an Earth House (2, 5 or 8) as Earth controls Water.

8 Mansions : This term refers to the 8 specific sections on the Bagua each having a direction. It is an aspect of Feng Shui that uses personal birth information and directional energy to determine a client's match to a home or building.

Concept : Each section on the Bagua Gua aligns with a universal principle and direction. In the 8 Mansions, Feng Shui directions play a major role when matching individuals with their personal directional energy.

24 Mountains : A term used to describe the breakdown of each of Bagua's 8 compass directions into 3 additional sections. When we multiply 3x8 it extends the Bagua into 24 sections.

Concept : There are subtle energy shifts within each of the 8 directions. If a direction is not particularly beneficial to a client, that direction is further divided into 3. Within this division there may be supportive energy within a non beneficial gua/section. There is a formula that shows exactly where this may lie. Micro siting these supportive areas is the purpose of the 24 mansions. A deeper layer of investigation that emphasizes how important directional energy is in Feng Shui.

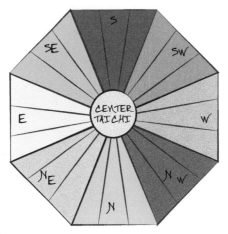

The 24 Mountains. Each of the 8 sections are divided.

Personal Directional Number and Element : Of the 8 directions on a Compass/Bagua, four will be optimal for any one person. Of these four one will stand out as your personal best. This direction has a number and element associated with it.

Concept : One's year of birth will determine the directions and elements for each individual. These four directions will align with an East or West grouping called East life or West life. This information is used to determine the best locations for one's orientation in a home or on land. Siting the main door and the head of a bed are areas of most importance in Feng Shui analysis. When a couple/partners differ in their groups, one should have the front door aligned with their group and the other individual the head of the bed aligned with their group. (the direction a head points to while asleep). These individual directions, and the ones that are optimal are often areas in a home or on land that an individual will feel best. A simple mathematical formula is used to determine a person's best direction, number and element.

Elemental Balance : The process of determining what elements make up an individual's Feng Shui birth chart in order to balance them in their environments. Birth chart information can be combined for a couple, family or members of a company to check what elements may be jointly shared or missing.

Elements that are missing or compromised are worked with to increase harmony within shared spaces or for an individual, family or group.

Concept : The Elemental Birth Chart alerts practitioners to missing elements so balance may be restored. This can be done from an interior or exterior viewpoint. External to a building, the animals in the landscape and their corresponding elements are checked. Corrections can be made before choosing building sites based on this practice.

East life : The term given to people born in the years when the energy arrived from one of four east directions.

West Life : The term given to people born in the years when the energy arrived or is most auspicious from the West directions.

Concept : Divided into two specific groups of four that align with East or West these two distinctions make up the eight directions on the Bagua compass. The East life directions are East, South East, North and South. West Life directions are West, South West, North West and North East.

Calculating West life or East life for clients allows a practitioner to focus on areas that may be problematic or challenging for them. Directional information determines how well a person aligns with a particular house or building. When examining the compass there are 3 directions in a group that are side by side with one removed from the group. This exemplifies the dynamic action of Yin moving towards Yang and vice versa. As seen in the Yin /Yang symbol there is always a bit of one within the other.

DIRECTIONAL ENERGY CALCULATION

STEP 1: **Add** the last two numbers of the Year of Birth 1973; 7+3 = 10

STEP 2: **Reduce** this number to a single digit 10; 1+0= 1

STEP 3: For WOMEN **add** this number to 5; 1+5 = 6

STEP 4: For MEN **subtract** this number from 10; 10 - 1 = 9

Find the number on the BAGUA to determine your direction;

For example #6 is in the **West**, thus this **woman** is **West Life (W, SW, W, NE) #9** is in the **South** ,thus this **man** is **East Life (E, SE, S, N)**

A male born in 1973 is East Life, his best direction is South, with supporting directions being East, Southeast and North. A woman born in 1973 is West Life; her best direction is West with supporting directions being Southwest, Northwest and Northeast

EXCEPTIONS:

- Nobody can have the **# 5** , as it sits in the center. **One more step** is required. If you get **# 5** and you are a woman you take the **# 8 NE** (West Life). If you are a man you take the **# 2 SW** (East life)

- When we find either sex born before February 4th of that year they may defer to the Directional energy of the year before. In most cases and depending on their Nine Star Ki directional energy, the date of the Chinese New Year determines the year used for this calculation.

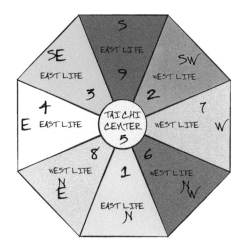

East Life and West Life directions and numbers.

In the interior of a building the balance can be restored with color, furnishings, layouts, lighting, and style. For example: If the interior of a home or a corporate building is found lacking the Metal element, there is the option to add it to the environment. Using metallic features, such as sculptures and archways, or adding the colors gold, silver or white will bring balance. These physical and visual additions create harmony by applying the Five Transformations or five element theroy.

Feng Shui Elemental Birth Chart©:
A chart that analyzes birth information to determine the elements present during the year, season, month, day and hour of birth.

Concept : Each individual's birth chart is unique. It allows a practitioner to use the Five Transformations to determine the overall elemental balance. The element of the year of birth (Chinese animal element) and the directional element are the two most important. For many practitioners these two are the only ones used in analysis. Nine Star Ki astrology is also used to determine elemental and personality traits. When elements are missing from a birth chart they can be introduced to create balance in a space or environment.

Lopan : The traditional Feng Shui Compass used by Feng Shui Master practitioners in China.

Concept : Traditionally illustrated in Chinese Calligraphy, it has moveable concentric circles that are manipulated by a Traditional Feng Shui Master. The layers and levels of information are gathered on site. Exact dates of birth, degrees of movement, the 8 Mansions, 24 Mountains, and other layers of astrological components of this fully functioning compass makes the Lopan a complex scientific tool.

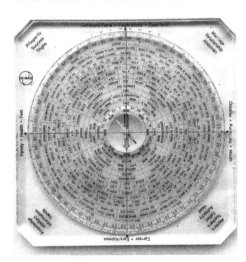

Modern Qi-Mag Lopan. Designed by Grand Master Jes Lim, it is transparent for placing directly on floor plans. The Lopan above is in English for ease of use in the West.

DIRECTIONAL ENERGY CHART: Example

A male, born on May 5, 1972, at 3:20 am would look like this: He is born in the year of the WATER Rat: The base element for Rat is WATER: He is born in a WOOD hour (between 3-5 am is Liver thus wood) : He is Influenced by western astrology. Taurus aligns with Snake which, as a Rat he is allotted the season winter which is WATER. And he is considered to be '# 1 WATER' as his directional element calculates as north (North in the magic square and on the Bagua is # 1 thus water) This male's Nine Star Ki numbers are based on the year, month and date of birth. Note that Principal numbers are easy to calculate, but the others require charts to calculate.

1 WATER (Principle #)

9 FIRE (Character #)

4 WOOD (Energetic #)

His missing elements would then be EARTH and METAL. These would be introduced into his home or work place if not intuitively added. A prominence of Water in his environment would indicate a major imbalance elementally. This often appears in a person's space as an abundance of an element they already have indicated in their chart. Elements are added in many ways through actual design details and features.

Cosmic Mouth of Chi : The location where the most powerful energy or atmospheric chi arrives at a home, building or piece of land. Atmospheric energy aligns with external site indicators such as a view, landscape features or the sun's energy. It can arrive by way of a roadway, landscape feature, a doorway or a window.

Concept : The Cosmic Mouth of Chi should align with an opening or entrance, as the energy arriving here is very auspicious and alive. Whether the entry be to an office building, a piece of land or a home. The cosmic mouth of Chi should align with the Energetic Front Door and Ming Tang. These terms may be used together, separately or interchangeably to describe a similar location, although they are ideas unto themselves.

Atmospheric Chi : The energy that arrives from the atmosphere that enriches our experience of a location or a building. It activates feelings of vitality.

Concept : The Cosmic Mouth of Chi is determined by investigating where the energy enters a space or piece of land. Sunlight, views and prevailing winds are contributing factors. The areas that are the most energized and alive are where the Atmospheric Chi is most powerful. When Atmospheric Chi aligns with a view it is considered a vital part of the Ming Tang.

Energetic Front Door : This is the area where the Atmospheric Chi arrives and enters a home, usually through a door or a window. It may be interchanged with the Cosmic Mouth of Chi.

Concept : This atmospheric energy is also known as cosmic energy that reaches us by way of the sun, the moon, wind, light or a breathtaking view. When it enters a main entrance of a home or business then that space is activated. The actual door or window is called Mouth of Chi and as such invites optimal health, wellbeing and prosperity to enter. When an architectural entry does not face the best atmospheric chi then finding the Cosmic Mouth of Chi is essential. It is determined by the location in the home or business that allows the most expansive view and most energized flow of nature to enter the space. This opening, whether it be a window or a door, is referred to as the Energetic Front Door.

Ming Tang : The literal translation of this Chinese term is 'great hall'. It is used to describe the view from a home. When it aligns with a main entrance or front door it simplifies Feng Shui investigations.

Concept : Ming Tang is used in Feng Shui to describe a view or space existing at the entry or energetic front door. The larger the Ming Tang the more Atmospheric Chi arrives at that location. The Ming Tang is often aligned with the Cosmic Mouth of Chi when the most auspicious energy arrives at this location. Ming Tang is measured in spatial and numerical dimensions from one to nine. The first is located just inside the energetic front door or main entry and is the size of a welcome mat. Each dimension gets exponentially larger as it moves from outside the door into the environment away from the house. In an urban setting the average Ming Tang measures 4 to 4.5 stopping at the door of the house across the street. When a home has a full Ming Tang it measures 1.5 kilometres of unlimited, unobstructed view. This is considered a full nine Ming Tang. The expansive energy that arrives from the cosmos, from both the sky and the land energizes a home. Symbolically it allows the occupants to see beyond the normal or expected. 'The million dollar view' and 'what you see is what you get' are phrases that illustrate the auspicious energy of Ming Tang in Feng Shui. An important consideration in Ming Tang is what the view features. Ming Tang is energized and richer when it is of a beautiful vista, as it allows life force energy to enter a home or a building. When a favourable Ming Tang or view is blocked or obscured, it symbolizes obstacles in the path of the occupants. Ming Tang is directly related to the Vision/South location on the Bagua when applying Landscape Feng Shui. When the main door does not align with a home's best Ming Tang, activating it will create positive and powerful Feng Shui.

Section Two gives a more integrated explanation of this concept in relationship to the schools of Feng Shui.

The Ming Tang from a 'back door' which is opposite the front door. It extends past 1.5 kilometres and captures a full nine Ming Tang. This view offers the Cosmic Mouth of Chi to external energy and although a back door it is considered 'The Energetic Front Door'.

11) Ming Tang is everywhere.

How to Activate an Energetic Front Door

Activation is a way of bringing intention and can be used to focus energy in a specific way. When a door or window has more powerful chi flow arriving from the outdoors, focusing attention there will activate it. This can be a window or door facing the best view not available at the architectural front door.

Recognizing where the most powerful energy arrives in a space is the first step in the activation process.

To activate is to spend more time at that particular window or use a door more frequently.

Standing in the space for a period of time each day and really absorbing the energy while envisioning what it is you see happening in your life or business is another step towards actualizing your goals thus activating the positive energy.

Qi-Mag International Feng Shui consultants use a special technique to activate doors, windows and semi-precious stones.

Every scenario is different. Some spaces may have to be activated by a professional in person or by distance activation. Generally shifting ones awareness towards realizing the power of the location can trigger the activation process without professional assistance.

The Heart Space : It is typically located at the center of a room, home, building or piece of land. It is related to the center of the Bagua in Feng Shui, which is called the Tai Chi or Sacred Center.

Concept : A mathematical formula puts the heart at the center of a space. This heart energy in Feng Shui is a metaphor for love and alignment with spiritual energy. It can shift energetically if the mathematical center is next to gathering spaces where humans share food and loving energy. What ever the location it should be kept clean, organized and well appointed. It is the best location to visibly display spiritual or religious objects and photos. This area of a building should not be disturbed by a stairway, fireplace or toilet. The Heart Space can also be found in more neutral locations such as hallways, circulation spaces and closets.

Locating And Understanding The Heart of A Space

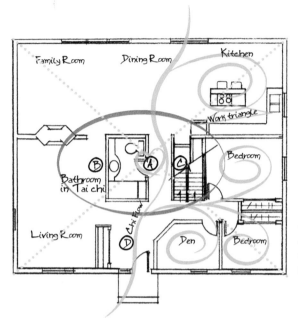

This illustration shows a home with several Feng Shui features worth noting; The Heart, Chi Flow and Pooling Chi.

A ~ The Heart of the home. The square shape of this home makes it easy to locate the center, which for all intents and purposes is considered the Heart location. Two lines drawn diagonally from corner to corner shows this location marked with an A.

B ~ A washroom located in the heart of a space compromises the energy. The heart should be an area of pooling chi. The water from the sink and toilet drain the vital energy needed in this area.

C ~ A stairway in the center directs energy upward and downward when located in the center or Heart. Chi is not able to pool in this situation. Also note the fireplace is not in the center. If located in the Tai Chi or Heart center, it would direct chi up, compromising the pooling chi needed here. These three features-washroom, stairway and fireplace should not be located in the center of any home.

D ~ The chi flow through the home follows a curvaceous path through the hallways and pools in the smaller rooms and kitchen. The chi does not however pool at the center or Heart due to the washroom and the stairwell.

Chi Flow Through A Residence

12) Section of a triple condo design done by author with land constrictions.

The energy /chi that flows into this lower floor is purposely directed and spills through the space naturally. The stairs are off to the side of the entry and far enough away so the energy is not initially directed towards them. The door opens into the fullness of the space. Chi flows in and around the circular shapes; table and counter. It then flows into the living area and onto the deck. The windows on the far wall are not directly across from the entry. This allows the energy and attention to stay in the space and circulate. Chi pools in various key areas allowing the immune system of occupants and guests to relax.

Pooling Chi : Areas where Chi or energy gathers or pools.
Concept : The concept of Pooling Chi when applied to design is the creation of spaces where occupants can sit, relax and gather with others without disturbances. An example would be a nook in a kitchen or the seating area in a living room. Pooling Chi areas create calmness and repose, allowing rejuvenation in homes, workspaces and designated areas. When circulation pathways run through sitting areas, the Chi is not able to pool. Designing with Pooling Chi in mind is often overlooked in modern design.

Tail of the Dragon : The name given to energy pathways that flow in gentle, curved, undulating lines rather than a direct one.

Concept : Chi should move as if it were following the tail of the dragon. This curvaceous flow allows Chi to take its time moving through space. When Chi flows too directly it can feel threatening. When slowed down it calms the immune system and allows a feeling of arrival or flow. Curved pathways create visual interest, promote relaxation and the observation of surroundings in a more conscious way. Energy flowing in this way nurtures harmony and beauty. Contrarily, long straight hallways, pathways or roadways accelerate Chi flow promoting anxiety, stress and danger.

14) Curved, undulating lines create a meandering flow of energy, referred to as the Tail of the Dragon. This photo shows it in the landscape with a dragon relief in the background.

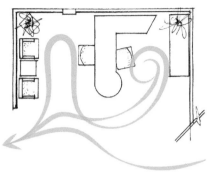

13) An open office concept illustrates good circulation between waiting area, work area and hallway circulation. It also shows Pooling Chi.

Circulation Space : The floor area assigned to hallways, stairways and exteriors pathways.

Concept: Optimally, Circulation Spaces should allow the Chi to flow in a gentle manner finding the Pooling Chi areas before continuing onwards. It is important that circulation spaces are well lit and free of blockages and clutter. The Tail of the Dragon creates good Circulation space and can lead to Pooling Chi areas. In large buildings with long hallways, Feng Shui cures such as mirrors and art work can slow down and direct Chi flow to be gentle and welcoming.

Landscape Feng Shui : Refers to the formations in the landscape based on the five elements. In Feng Shui, leaning how to read them will inform how they can affect us. The term does not refer to landscaping per se, but can be applied to landscape design. It is also associated with Form School Feng Shui.

Concept : It is used to locate the most auspicious formations found in the landscape for the placement of buildings. Landscape Feng Shui uses the five elements and relates to geo-physical forms In the environment. It can be juxtaposed over the physical body, a desk, room, house, piece of land or a city. As a basic principle of Form School Feng Shui, balanced and auspicious land formations take precedent over Compass School or Directional Energy. When these formations are in the most powerful positions they have a dynamic affect on occupants. The five elements are recognized in the environment by way of shape, size, color and location. They indicate where energized and beneficial locations exist when developing land and placing buildings. Landscape Feng Shui is also used to recognize power spots.

Compass School : Also known as the Traditional School of Feng Shui, it places its primary emphasis on the compass directions and the energies that are associated with each direction of the Feng Shui Compass or Bagua.
Concept : The Compass was developed in China as a form of divination used to tune into geomagnetic energies of the earth. Used as far back as the Sung Dynasty, the compass was created for areas that had no form in the landscape. The Chinese used magnetite to attune with magnetic and geomantic forces underground. Flatlands, waterways and atmospheric conditions relayed information which eventually led to the evolution of the more complex Lopan in Feng Shui Practice. Traditional Feng Shui is based on the layers of information gathered to determine auspicious locations. Traditional Compass School and Form School emerged at the same time yet in different locations of China. Both schools are valid and practiced world wide, often in conjunction with each other.

Form School : The school of Feng Shui that places its emphasis on the forms in the landscape; predominately in mountainous or hilly regions. These forms are related to animals and symbology in Feng Shui for auspicious placement. In North America, Form School is the theory primarily used in the Black Hat School of Feng Shui.
Concept : In Form School Feng Shui, animals align with the five elements which are placed within geophysical features. Compass directions are acknowledged but used so that South is aligned with the sun or the view (Ming Tang). Landforms are observed according to prominent features such as waterways, plateaus, mountain passes, etc. Form School is a part of the Traditional Compass School, as it holds valuable information pertinent to Feng Shui investigations. In North America, Feng Shui was introduced by Master Lin Yun who named it The Black Hat Sect of Feng Shui.

Black Hat Sect Feng Shui : An interpretation of Feng Shui that is aligned with Tibetan Buddhism specific to the Bon Sect.
Concept : Form School has been applied primarily in North America through the teachings of Master Thomas Lin Yun, who came to North America in the late 60's. He brought the more mystical teachings of the Tibetan Bon Black Hat Sect to the West. Since that time its become a known and common method of practicing Feng Shui in North America and other parts of the western world. This interpretation uses a spiritual approach with Form School and the 3 Door System as the core of methodology.

The Black Hat Feng Shui eliminates the more complex Compass School practice (Traditional Compass School) thus making it more accessible for Western Application.

3 Door System : The placement of North on the side of the building where the main entrance is located. The entry door is either on the right, in the middle or on the left, thus the term 3 door. The exact location dictates what meaning is assigned to each of these 3 directions.

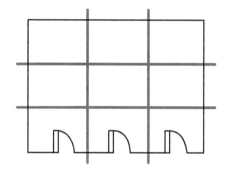

A front door will be located in one of 3 places on the facing of a building; left, center or right.

Concept : The 3 Door System is a definitive part of Form School Feng Shui. It is however the primary practice of the Black Hat Sect of Feng Shui. In Traditional Feng Shui it is used as a check point and is combined with Form and Compass school theory to determine the overall energy in an environment.

Power position : The location in a room, home or piece of land that has optimal Feng Shui. It is where the physical body is relaxed yet observant of all that is around.

Concept : The model for finding a power position is in understanding Landscape Feng Shui and how it applies to the body. Good body landscape creates good backing and optimal visual awareness. Power positions can be one or more locations in a room, a building or on land.

Power Position in an Office Space

The power position affords ultimate visual access to all in the surroundings while providing good backing and relaxation. It allows the immune system to be completely at rest. Power positions create inner well being thus supports our power source.

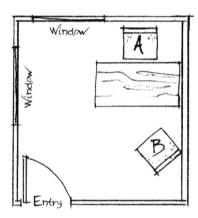

A) Are power positions. They have good Landscape Feng Shui and offer a protected back and good visual access.

B) Are not power positions as they lack or have insufficient backing which creates unease.

C) Placed in the least favourable position as there is no 'backing', even though chair C has good visibility.

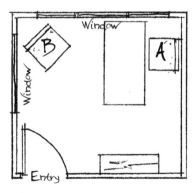

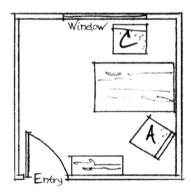

Anchor position : This is a location that anchors the energy of a home or a building.

Concept : Although the anchor and the power position can be the same at times they are not always. The office of a CEO should be an anchor position for a corporation and the CEO's office location in the building should be in a power position. A master bedroom that is located away from the front door and closer to the rear of a home is an anchor position for a home but not necessarily a power position. Typically energy should be more active in a workplace than a home so these terms shift in application.

Dowsing : An ancient method of divination commonly practiced to find naturally occurring underground water.

Concept : Dowsing is used to locate geophysical and metaphysical energies. Dowsing is also used to determine the location of minerals and unseen subterranean energies. Dowsers use intuition, intention and a dowsing tool to seek specific energies. Dowsing tools are varied around the world. In the west pendulums, forked sticks or metal dowsing rods are common. The tool acts as an extension of the body's awareness, which connects with the energy of what ever is being sought. Dowers have been finding water for millennia.

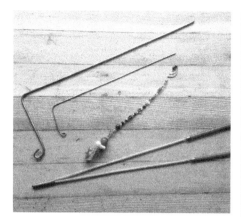
Dowsing Tools

Dowsing Protocol : This is a set of questions asked before dowsing. These questions are asked as a check in to affirm that he or she can obtain effective answers.

Concept : It is the job of a dowser to tune into energy and to be clear while doing so. This requires the ability to get out of one's head or intellect and tune into the subtle energy fields around them. It is important that a dowser must be objective and leave subjective interpretation out of his quest for information. The protocol questions are: may I? should I? or can I? Affirmative answers by the use of muscle testing or dowsing tools are used to ask these questions. Following protocol is imperative when working on someone's behalf.

Geomancy : The study of natural occurring subterranean earth energy and its effects on humans,

Author using dowsing rod in a garden space.

animals and locations.

Concept : Geomancy is a process of gathering information from our environment. This information comes from geophysical, metaphysical or electromagnetic sources. Geophysical energies range from naturally occurring water, microwave energies, gamma radiation, fault lines and the convergence of water in a fault line. Metaphysical energy is usually human influenced such as burial sites, ceremonial grounds and war zones. The understanding and use of geomancy helps the dowser to find safe and favourable areas for building sites. Subterranean geophysical, metaphysical and electromagnetic energies have been known to create stress and illness. Geomantic dowsers are able to detect such unfavourable locations and advise builders and developers how to avoid them. Some dowsers are able to energetically clear and block unhealthy energies to eliminate or divert negative affects.

Human Memory Imprint: An unseen energy left behind by human activity in any given location.

15) Location of a major geomantic 'Ley Line'.

Concept : There are many forms of human memory imprint; some are positive and some are difficult to be around. When a happy event takes place in a location, it may linger for a time and be felt by those around it. When difficult or tragic events occur, these too leave a memory imprint. Humans respond in various ways to these imprints depending on personal sensitivity. Locations such as graves, murder scenes or epidemic death sites will affect sensitive types while others

may feel nothing. This term is used in geomantic clearing work when dowsing land and buildings for metaphysical information.

Ley Line : Energy lines that connect locations of special significance to each other. They form on the earth surface and are created from repetitive human and animal use. **Concepts** : A simple Ley Line is an animal track. Animal's intuitive senses take them safely from one place to another. Over time the energetic imprint can be followed by other animals even if these lines are not visual. They are also activated energy lines that connect or align places of power. They are viewed by some as mystical alignments that connect special locations. In Britain many cathedrals are built on power spots, often used by the Druids before the Roman invasions. These locations have been found to be connected by old Ley Lines.

Geopathic Stress : Natural subterranean earth energies that can cause harm to humans and animals.
Concept : Geopathic stress can be caused by the effects of multiple subterranean energies. The most profound or strongest are microwave and gamma radiations. They emit from underground streams, mineral concentrations, fault lines and subterranean

water courses. While resting, we rejuvenate the immune system so that it can fight infections, absorb nutrients and replenish our energy reserves. When Geopathic Stress is present, the immune system is at risk. Sleeping free from Geopathic Stress is optimal for good health. Geopathic stress points can severely affect health when they are lived over for extended periods. Illnesses such as cancer, chronic fatigue syndrome, infertility and miscarriages can result. In Europe, these phenomena are widely researched and linked to Geopathic stress. Doctors will inquire about a

Human memory imprints are not always visible like these small momentos left at the grave site of a young pilot.

patient's house location and in some instances visit a patient's home to check for Geopathic and other stressful influences. In the Americas this practice is rare in allopathic medicine.

A geomantic dowser can find the location of fault lines and water lines that run near homes or under potential building sites. The information is useful when developing land or when trying to determine if there are disturbances at an existing location. The illustration shows a major subterranean fault that lay directly under the entrance. A complication is a water source that has found the fault/fissure and has changed course to flow in the fault line.

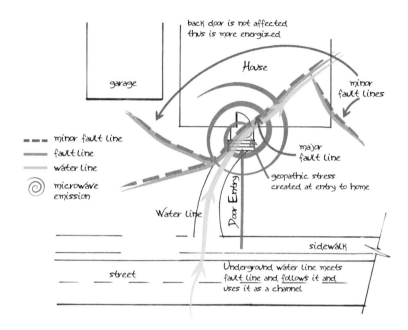

Although fault lines and naturally occurring water lines are a frequent ordinary phenomena, when they are found near or under buildings they can create disturbances. This is known as geopathic stress. This stress can prevent energy from flowing into or circulating in a space causing dis-ease for occupants. This illustration shows an actual Feng Shui client investigation.

Metaphysical stress : Stress caused by detrimental human activity such as war, epidemics and sudden death. It is often human memory imprint left behind due to suffering and disturbed emotional energy. In nature it is found both above and below ground. It can be detected in buildings with notable history.

Concept : Sensitive people can feel disturbed energy intuitively or if dowsing specifically for its presence. For the public in general it can be overwhelming

HOW GEOMANCY AFFECTS DESIGN AND DEVELOPMENT

In the design and development professions, proper siting is step one of the process. Many factors are considered: the sun's path, access, land topography, garden sites, soil conditions and what is adjacent in the environment. Basic to all development is water. In rural areas, water sources are crucial. Water witching and dowsing for wells is a common and ancient art. Water is one of the many geomantic influences to be considered for new development and building sites.

Geopathic disturbances can create problems for humans when they live above them for long periods of time. Signs to watch for are lack of sleep or too much, reoccurring disease and mental stress. Ancient and current nomadic cultures have used geomantic practices for millennia as a matter of logic and common sense.

For developers, builders, architects and clients, awareness of these energies can act as a warning for potential problems. It can also save time and resources should areas not be favorable to develop. In Feng Shui Design, geomancy is an important part of balanced and harmonious environments.

to come across areas that hold Metaphysical stress. It occurs when trees have been cut down without permission, or natural areas denigrated. This is believed to create disturbed nature spirits. Power spots on the planet that have high frequencies caused by minerals or crystals are considered metaphysical but are not stressful.

Underground : Everything that is under the earth's crust or subterranean.

Concept : Underground in this text will refer to natural geophysical and metaphysical phenomena. From a Feng Shui Design perspective it informs us of energies that affect human occupancy of land and buildings.

Underground Geomantic Phenomena : What takes place underground that has an influence on human activity above it.

Concept : Should a vertical subterranean cross section be taken at any point on the earth's surface it will reveal layers of history. These stacked layers reveal both metaphysical and geophysical phenomena that can be dowsed for above ground. Many metaphysical influences are created by human action. Geo-physical influences are earth features that have formed our planet, layer upon layer. Human influenced developments such as mining, drilling or excavating that may have been dormant can become reactivated when disturbed. This also occurs due to natural phenomena such as earthquakes and volcanoes. Dowsing is an effective way of checking areas to detect anomalies in the land before development begins.

Natural gamma ray emissions : A naturally occurring electromagnetic phenomena, both solar and subterranean. When underground, this radiation is released by the decay of radioisotopes and causes ionization which can be harmful to humans.

Concept : Gamma Ray radiation can be found in high concentrations emanating from cut banks in the earth. Buildings erected close to these areas may have high concentration of gamma ray emissions thus affecting occupants. It also emanates from seismic activity and fault lines in lesser concentrations.

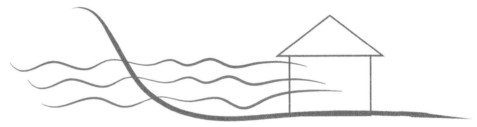

Gamma radiation can result in cut banks in the earth to allow for building.

Natural Microwave emissions : A natural occurring phenomena created by water flow being restricted underground.

Concept : Water seeks fault lines and crevices to flow into. Should these crevices be narrow, the restricted water will back up and form an eddy. This phenomena can send Microwave emissions to the earth's surface in spiraling waves. These microwaves can add stress to the immune system and overall health if the exposure is for long periods. However when exposure to natural occurring microwave energy is in small doses or for short periods it can have an energizing influence. In design, placing a bed above this phenomena would be more harmful than placing toilets over such areas due to the amount of time spent there.

Sound pollution : A modern day term for multiple sources of noise at a constant, uncomfortable or distracting volume.

Concept : In cities one may get used to multiple sources of sound, but for those with high sensitivities to noise it is considered sound pollution. Humans who experience it unconsciously may also deal with negative affects. Insufficient attention is given to materials that are effective in eliminating echo effects and high volume in home, work and public spaces. Internal heating and cooling systems that are not well considered or insulated from sleeping areas create sound pollution.

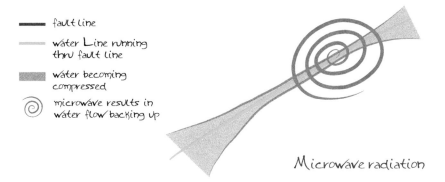

fault line

water Line running thru fault line

water becoming compressed

microwave results in water flow backing up

Microwave radiation

Activation : To convert from an inactive or dormant form into an active form. Applied to a wide variety of concepts, in this text it will refer to a shift in consciousness, a shift in space or the activation of stones and land.
Concept : In Feng Shui it is the process of becoming aware and embracing new ideas and concepts. Activation allows us to move beyond preconceived limitations and can lead to an immediate shift in one's reality. In its most esoteric sense it is the magic of Feng Shui intention and manifestation. Activation in a geomantic sense refers to physically activating dormant energy, whether this be in a stone or an entire piece of land. Activating techniques are often used with dowsing tools and geomantic practices.

Orientation : To get one's bearings.
Concept : In Feng Shui the compass is used to orient the Bagua and subsequent energies on a piece of land or a building. The process of following compass directions is to orient oneself.

I Ching : Also known as the book of changes, the I Ching is one of the oldest Chinese classics dating back to 1000-500 BC. Its use evolved over several periods as a philosophical and divination tool. It has inspired eastern art, literature, religious and social commentary. Used widely in the East for centuries, it is now known world wide and consulted for guidance and moral decision making. It is considered the foundational text for Taoism and Confucian ideologies.
Concept : The I Ching uses a series of three solid/ yang lines and three broken/yin lines to represent a family of eight. The family members are father, mother and oldest, middle and youngest males and females. These 8 Trigrams can be arranged in 8 ways giving us 64 combinations. Yarrow sticks or Chinese coins are tossed to determine which of the possible 64 combinations will answer the question of a seeker of I Ching wisdom. In Feng Shui each of the 8 trigrams or family members is assigned a direction on the Bagua. Each trigram/ direction aligns with a universal energy. When the Bagua is placed on a home, building or a piece of land the energy present in a specific direction relates to I Ching wisdom. In Feng Shui this information is used to assist one to help create harmony and balance in an environment.

Tao : The Path or the Way, the Tao is the observation of 'what is'.
Concept : The Tao is the simple observation of natural phenomena in our environments. Associated with Confucianism and Buddhist ideology, it seeks to create awareness of all that is

so we can respond to circumstance without drama.

Feng Shui Cure : This is a remedy used to bring attention to an area needing adjustment. A Feng Shui cure may work indefinitely or need 'reactivation' depending on what it is used for.

Concept : The concept and use of cures is very much alive in the various schools of Feng Shui. Often associated with superstition, cures are created to bring awareness to a situation that needs shifting. It serves as a reminder to create a positive outcome through intention. Placing an object or cure will not automatically change a condition. The use of energized or high frequency crystals or semi precious stones can carry intention and shift energy when used for this purpose. Traditional Feng Shui cures are meant to shift chi flow when it needs to be to activated or redirected. The placement of crystals, mirrors, lighting and other modern decor items can be used as cures when one is aware of their power, use and intention.

Sacred Geometry : Geometric features found in nature that exhibit intricate patterns and proportions. Snowflakes are an example of infinite mathematical combinations, each having balance, harmony and beauty. Sacred Geometry is applied

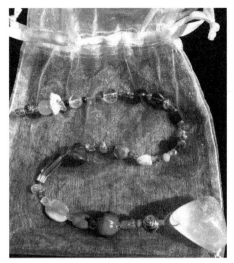

Quartz Crystal is used in Feng Shui to clear energy, activate intentions and bring life to stagnant areas.

to architecture and design around the globe.

Concept : Patterns in nature evoke awe. As holistic and holographic expressions of life they have been used in design to reflect the Divine thus the term Sacred Geometry. Applied to architecture it exhibits the very essence of Feng Shui, creating spaces that resonate deeply with the human psyche. Leonardo De Vinci's Vetruvian man stands in both a square and a circle. It illustrates what he believed to be the workings of the human body as an analogy for the workings of the universe. Geometrical shapes, such as the flower of life, have been superimposed over his sketches to show how geometric proportions work. As another example, the

golden mean, found most commonly in a sea shell has been taught in all design programs world wide. Feng Shui Design recognizes sacred geometry as an integral mirroring of the natural world.

Moon Gate : A moon gate is a circular opening, usually to a garden that acts as a passageway. Once a denoting class status, this traditional Chinese architectural feature is found world wide as a symbol of beauty.

Concept : Originally built with spiritual connotations, it remains today a Feng Shui symbol of consciously shifting from one level of awareness to another.
See page 105.

A Traditional Chinese moon gate has a tiled roof and the circle opening stops short to allow a walk through.

GEOMANCY: Its Roots, History and Use

Geomancy can be traced historically to Asia, its knowledge brought back by the Arabs along the ancient Silk Road. The term Geomancy is from the Latin word 'geomanteria' which translates as foresight by earth, and the Arabic term 'ilm alrami' or the science of the sand.

Geomancy today extends to not just the geo-physical but to metaphysical and electromagnetic influences and how they affect health and well being.

The information derived from geomantic investigation can inform us of a variety of unseen energies; from areas of potential hazard to power spots. Awareness of Geomancy in the design and development world has more than practical applications when finding land suitable for human habitation. With the variety of subterranean influences affecting our natural and man made environments, dowsing and geomantic practices are being acknowledged with a fresh perspective.

Radon gas is one example of a natural geophysical phenomena that can have fatal effects for those living near or above its emissions. Radon detectors are widely used in the Americas.

There are many subterranean energies that are not detected by the human eye. A trained geomancer can visually spot areas as well as dowse for them. Some visual clues for observing geomantic phenomena include

- areas of grass discolouration or unusual depressions in flat land.

- Cracks in cement that reoccur even when repaved or fixed

- Abnormal growth patterns in plants and trees

The pull of a subterranean waterway close to the earth's surface can affect all matter of flora and fauna. Seismic activity can show in the earth's surface, in areas of major fault lines.

Metaphysical influences are less understood as they have a more mysterious nature and are subjective to the one perceiving them. Sometimes felt more than actually observed, metaphysical disturbances are best dowsed for with specific protocols and questions. War zones or places of human tragedy are types of metaphysical energy that can be problematic if the land above these areas are disturbed for human development. Other high energy spots such as Stonehenge, are also metaphysical yet affect us. Power spots can be visual or invisible to the eye but visceral to the senses. Man and animals are deeply sensitive to the effects of these types of geomantic influences.

Electromagnetic or EMF (electromagnetic radiation) is a relatively new phenomena as it pertains to the man made electronic world. Other electromagnetic energy such as naturally occurring gamma ray and microwave radiation on the other hand are an intricate part of the planet's makeup.

It is important to note here that geomantic energy can lay dormant for years. Human based development or environmental changes can reactivate undetected areas, affecting human and animal life. Tornados, tsunamis, wildfires and earthquakes, although geophysical in nature can create metaphysical activation.

The study of land formations for geomantic anomalies is a learned art.

Misshapen trees are often following an underground water line. A trained eye will recognize this anomaly as geophysical stress.

16) A rock formation sits in an open vast space in the foothills of the Rocky Mountain range. Geophysical features like this are acknowledged as noteworthy sites, visited by many.

Author's Geomantic Bio

Meeting a geomantic Feng Shui master seven years into my study deepened my fascination with the work. It introduced me to the unseen world of energy which impacts all space. Feng Shui conceptualized the importance of energy flow in design, and what we feel that is not seen. Learning that geophysical, metaphysical and electromagnetic energies influence all space led to my expanded awareness of the design world.

Often we are born in locations and with gifts that affect our lives yet take a lifetime to understand and appreciate. Cape Breton Island, where I grew up, had very distinct geophysical anomalies. The island features both a salt and fresh water lake system at its centre, or the heart of the island. Islands are normally surrounded by water, not filled with it. The island also featured miles of underground mining shafts, from coal mines which reached far out under the Atlantic Ocean. Many islanders who lived close to coal seams located their homes above them, digging underground and using the coal as a heat source until the 1950's. This was the case with my family home. What resulted was a labyrinth of underground tunnels in the more industrial and populated areas.

In my twenties I spent nine years in Canada's Arctic working as a Facility Programmer for the Government of the Northwest Territories. Travelling into the vastness of this land and ascribing minimal square footage space to client departments seemed odd if not ridiculous at times. It was later, when I started to study geomancy that the geographic anomalies of my birth island and my experiences in Northern Canada started to make sense.

Before that awakening and having left the Arctic, I travelled and spent several years between Latin America and Asia. During these trips I sensed how culture and land mass shaped peoples' perspective. When pregnant with my first child I chose to live in a mountain town in British Columbia. Although I had purchased land in coastal BC, I felt more comfortable raising my children in the shelter of the mountains. With family far away, they acted as the ones holding me. It was only after my second child was born that I read my first book on Feng Shui. Reading it cover to cover in one evening I understood its principles intuitively and so started this journey. Only years later did I realize how I was informed and guided by landscapes. Geomancy can have a huge impact on our experiences, psychic and understanding.

Sacred Geometry as it relates to Feng Shui

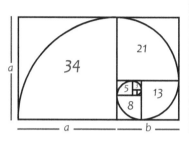
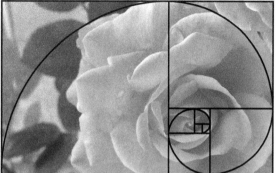

Golden Mean and Fibonacci Series

Sacred Geometry, Feng Shui and Design

17) *Sacred geometry is found in thousands of cathedrals around the world.*

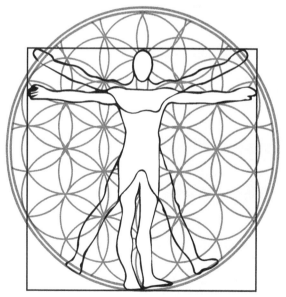

De Vinici's Vetruvian Man is overlaid with the Tree of Life which is considered sacred geometry.

Ngurah Rai Airport in Den Passar

Traditional meets the modern at Ngurah Rai Airport, Bali, Indonesia. Expansive rooflines combined with ancient cultural decor evokes wonder: the essence of Feng Shui Design.

Good design is Good Feng Shui

18) 1970's Vancouver condo renovation followed the buildings retro style and client's zen yearnings. Finding original hardwood floors, with a variation of patterns helped define spaces. The zen and retro allowed a simple, clean Feng Shui design solution.

FENG SHUI THEORY: The Elements, Schools and the Bagua Compass

How the elements relate to all professions in Feng Shui

The Elements shape who we are. They are at the very core of creation. The words Feng~wind and Shui~water attest to this. Our breath (Feng) and water (Shui) are what sustains us; these Chinese words express our very essence. Feng Shui is about how human nature interacts and depends on our environment and our ultimate placement therein. To that end, linking specific design and development professions to the elements is a valuable tool. It also offers deeper understanding for all walks of life.

Feng Shui design and indeed all Feng Shui theory stems from the interpretation of the the Five Transformations or the Five Element theory. Exploring each one separately allows us to understand their personality and attributes and how they relate to us individually. There is a simplicity and an appropriateness in assigning each of the Elements to the various design and development disciplines. It is the same with us as individuals as we generate a dominant energy and impulse. Rarely are there careers that exhibit elemental characteristics equally. The objective in this section is to decode the characteristics that predominate personal impulses in life and our career choices. It is also to share the basics of Feng Shui Schools and thinking so readers can better understand its relevance both in the past and in modern application.

The Five Elements

Fire
(Fire is the child of Wood, the parent of Earth & the grandparent of Metal)

Fire as in Architecture is visual and dynamic. It seeks to be seen and noticed.
ARCHITECTS = creativity, being seen, spokespersons, dramatic

Earth
(Earth is the child of Fire, parent of Metal & the grandparent of Water)

Earth as in Building is solid and strong; it needs to be rooted and dependable.
BUILDERS = working with earth, starting from the ground up

Metal
(Metal is the child of Earth, the parent of Water & grandparent of Wood)

Metal as in Development is direct, solid and concise. It is creative and compliant
with a definitive result as a completion point.
DEVELOPERS = leaders, in control, responsible for the overall

Water
(Water is the child of Metal, the parent of Wood and the grandparent of Earth)

Water as in Design is a deep and thoughtful process. It processes information and
carefully allows it to flow to express a look, feeling and a solution to given criteria.
DESIGNERS = Fluid, creative, unpredictable, many faceted, deep

Wood
(Wood is the child of Water, parent of Fire & the grandparent of Earth)

Wood is movement and direction. It is felt, noticed and often predictable.
DECORATORS = visionary, ideas, movement, birth & rebirth

EAST VS WEST
Four Elements and Five Elements

The Five Elements of the Five Transformations bear resemblance to what we know in Europe and North America as the Four Elements; Fire, Earth, Air and Water. In Asian theory the fifth element results when you split the element Air into its two essential aspects; giving us Wood and Metal. The essence of Air is required with Fire to melt Metal. In the creating of Metal there is a mystical aspect of the alchemic process which turns base metals into gold. Air is an essential part of this transformation. Wood uses Air to change carbon dioxide into oxygen. With this expansion to a fifth element there is now a central position which anchors the four, Earth at the center with the other four at a cardinal direction. The five elements coincide with our five senses and in doing so relate to our bodily experiences and makes them sensual in their presentation. All cultures have sought to understand the elements from ancient Babylonia & Greece through to the alchemists of Medieval times. The Persians were the first to apply elemental knowledge to garden design which then migrated along the Silk Road. We witness this now in the beauty of the Tao and Zen gardens. The five elements are at the core of the traditional Asian medicine of Tibet & China. The Hindu culture names ether as the fifth element which Tibetans call 'energy or space'. Both refer to the essentialness which is Air. The basic nature of these five elements can be applied to human impulses as in our personalities and our professions.

The Five Transformations in Feng Shui Design

THE THEORY

The five elements are Fire, Earth, Metal, Water, and Wood. Chi has two basic distinctions, Yin and Yang. The elements express the dynamic relationship of Yin and Yang as they move from one to the other. Yin carries a bit of Yang within and vice versa. This process, called the Five Transformations, is key to the balance of all Yin and Yang energies within the body and the planet.

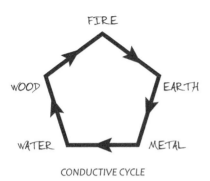

CONDUCTIVE CYCLE

Elemental interaction has two distinctive cycles; the CONDUCTIVE cycle and the CONTROLLING cycle. The clockwise arrows move in a 'circular' pattern; this is the conductive cycle. The arrows on the inside form a 'star' pattern which indicates the controlling cycle. These patterns will show up in other illustrations in this book. The more the pattern is recognized the deeper the understanding. The five pointed star shape is easily used as a reminder of both cycles.

CONTROL CYCLE

The CONDUCTIVE Cycle

This is the beneficent and assisting cycle of the elemental relationship.

From FIRE we get EARTH
Fire reduces everything to ashes; that which creates and nurtures Earth.

From EARTH we get METAL
Deep within the Earth lies Metal and all Metal is extracted from it.

From METAL we find WATER
This is a symbolic as well as a physical relationship. Traditionally gold and silver were the containers for Water. Metal, like Water, becomes a liquid when melted.

From WATER we get WOOD
Water is necessary for Wood to grow. From rain, dew or mist come the flourishing of all plant life.

From WOOD we get FIRE
Wood needs Fire to burn. The friction of rubbing sticks together with tinder creates Fire.

The CONTROLLING Cycle

In order to achieve balance these elements have an opposite and equal challenge or control.

FIRE is controlled by WATER
Water can immediately extinguish Fire.

WATER is controlled by EARTH
Water is absorbed by Earth. Earth can direct the flow of Water.

EARTH is controlled by Wood
Wood displaces Earth and uses it as nourishment.

WOOD is controlled by METAL
Metal cuts Wood.

METAL is melted by FIRE.
Metal softens under Fires intensity.

The flow of the energy within these two cycles show that no element is stronger or weaker. Each has its place in the chain of life and are constantly seeking Balance. Like Yin and Yang, all elements are equal and interdependent yet dynamically in motion.

AUTHORS FENG SHUI JOURNEY

My journey with Feng Shui was influenced by a design background. Interior Design taught me to be as close to an architectural thinker as possible; inquisitive, open and clear. Feng Shui directs us towards understanding what energies lie in all spaces. I wanted to know where to place a compass to know more about the directions that influence Career, Relationships, Health and all points on the Bagua. It became important that my work reflect the understanding of these concepts; not just to shift aesthetics, but to influence energy flow. Initially Feng Shui led me to the study of the Bagua or Feng Shui compass. With tremendous enthusiasm I read my first Feng Shui book in one sitting in 1993 and I was hooked. It was not until seven years into my Feng Shui Design practise, under the tutelage of two teachers that I felt my work had peaked. Experience had taught me much but I had a feeling that I was not as effective as I wanted to be. My design work was good but the energy in spaces were less than I expected. At that time I met Dr. Jes Lim, the teacher who would become my primary Feng Shui Master. He urged all of his students to go back to the basics, to look at the simple things and not to overlook the primary aspects that give Feng Shui its ultimate credibility.

He focused on Landscape Feng Shui; the root of what we call Form School and the impulse behind the 3 Door System. He introduced the Five Elements in a different way than I had been previously taught. He trained us to look at the 'core elements' present in a client's birth chart and not to ever do anything that would jeopardize them, thus personalizing the work.

Creating a practical guide to assist others and share my knowledge seemed important. A text without theory overload could serve as a simple reference. When I started my practise there was a great deal of confusion about basic concepts and the different schools of Feng Shui. It was clear that it had be based on core human impulses which stemmed from knowing the elementals. Wind/Feng and Water/ Shui are basic to human nature. Integrating these ideas and concepts into modern design would allow us to be comfortable and secure in all our environments. As my Feng Shui Design career expanded, working with the unseen world of energy in spaces and landscapes was a natural step. Geomancy speaks to the planetary and human unseen energies that affect landscapes and buildings. By integrating the visual aesthetics with energetic imprints I was

able to understand fully what happens when man impacts the environment.

"There is no logical way to discover of these elemental laws. There is only the way of Intuition, which is helped by a feeling for the order lying behind appearance."

The mystery behind Einstein's quote inspired me to years of study and interpretation. What started as a reference manual for design and development professions has evolved into a guide for anyone wanting to know more about the essence of who we are and how to create harmony and health.

ELEMENTAL INFLUENCES ON THE BODY

Each of the five elements is connected to an organ or a group of organs. Fire controls the circulatory system including the heart and the 3 heart pumps known as the triple heater. Earth controls the spleen, pancreas, and stomach. Metal controls the lungs, skin and colon. Water controls the kidneys, bladder and reproductive system. Wood controls the liver and gall bladder.

Chinese and Tibetan medical practitioners and herbalists work with balancing the chi flow in the body. Meridians are the conduit of energy for each organ within its respective element. When chi flow is weak in one organ, it will in turn affect the energy of other related organs. For example, if a Wood related organ is weak (liver or gall bladder) it will affect one or more of the Earth organs and so on. When all organs are strong they work to support each other. The ideal is to balance the Controlling or Supportive cycle at work within the body.

The Five Transformations are a way of viewing how the entire system has a domino effect, both within the body and in the environment. Feng Shui is investigative work that uncovers imbalances and seeks to correct them outside the body. The five elemental theory is only one part of the multilayered onion that Feng Shui reveals. It is core, however, in understanding how this ancient art has endured.

Feng Shui theory and the Five Transformations become more intriguing when we can relate them to professions. The impulse behind each element affects our choice of careers and can awaken a new awareness within our environments.

PROFESSIONAL DISCIPLINES & THE FIVE TRANSFORMATIONS

The fundamental essence of what we do is born out of the elements in our personal makeup. The ones that predominate will lead us to an occupation or profession that allows us to express our true nature. The five elements distinguish characteristics that define and shape our choices.

A previous illustration groups various walks of life into specific elements. Each element has a personality type that can be determined by using birth information. Recognizing your impulses within the following may assist you to better understand what you do and what you attract. Careers such as Architecture, Development, Building, Interior Design and Decoration are intrinsically interrelated; much like the five elements. I choose to get specific in exploring these creative professions as they have the most impact in manifesting exceptional Feng Shui Design.

Elemental understanding expands into every aspect of our lives and as such is the very essence of Feng Shui. How we respond to the elemental characteristics creates a perspective and depth of understanding. The elements reveal not only career choices but can inform us about health, compatibility in relationships and what spiritual practices we align with. In essence, the elements reveal information about all that surrounds us.

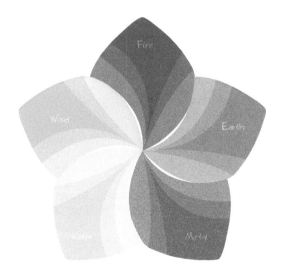

Fire

FIRE

ARCHITECTS and FIRE

Fire as in Architecture is visual and dynamic. It seeks to be seen and noticed.

19) FIRE is located in one area only of the Bagua compass.

It is visible, dynamic, visionary and is represented by the Trigram for FIRE (S).

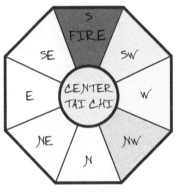

FIRE LIVES IN THE SOUTH ONLY

FIRE SHAPE

21) Fire in architecture is both the color red and the angle of the extension. Lighting is also fire in the building.

The Fire Element

(Fire is the child of Wood, the parent of Earth & the grandparent of Metal)

Fire is fast moving and decisive. It is known as a purifier. All but the base elements are burned away by Fire and symbolically the truth is left exposed. Fire has an explosive quality, both visual and alluring. There is a peak to fire activity, just as noon is the highest energetic point of the day. Fire is the expression of Yang energy at its apex that eventually declines and softens. Fire burns out if not fed by the element Wood. Fire's location is South, the hours leading to and just after noon are its time of day and summer its time of year. Sunshine, heat, passion and all aspects of life that are vibrant, engaging and spark our imaginations are considered Fire. It symbolizes vision, fame and community standing. It is found on the Bagua in the South only and is represented by the Trigram Li; two solid Yang lines holding a broken Yin line.

In Design Fire is present as lighting, the color red, live animals, photographs of loved ones and original art works. It is also represented as collections of inspiring books and music, as they hold a passionate connection for their owner. Symbolically Fire includes triangles, peaked roofs and furniture that is arranged on angles.

It is the color red and red purple only.

In the landscape Fire is best represented in Mountains with pronounced peaks that stand alone. Steeples of churches are layered with the symbolism of Fire. Both angular and pointing up, they represent where we look for vision and divine guidance.

Architecture is a visual expression of Fire. The Fire Element is expressed through the power of visuals and making a statement. Passion, vision and energy go into creating impactive architecture, especially on a grand scale. Therein lies the essence of what Fire represents. The Guggenheim Museums in NY and Spain, the Empire State Building and the Sagrada Familia are examples of how powerful architecture shines and illuminates our vision.

Human Characteristics : People who have #9 Fire as their Nine Star Ki Principle number are visionaries. They are often the spokesperson for groups as they have the skill set to convey ideas that need to be heard. These people are the doers; they are dynamic in their presentation and visibly stand out. Fire personalities do not fear taking risks. As Fire is related to the heart and circulation system we find that Fire people put their hearts into all they do. This can present as greed, impulsiveness and a lack of consideration. Generally outspoken, Fire types must cultivate their abilities to listen. On the other hand, when a Fire person is muted or unheard, depression ensues. Cultivating compassion for all perspectives is key to Fire personalities. Being able to maintain subtle control is a key factor for balancing Fire. Those who can manifest a vision embody the very core of this element. Clothing designers, makeup artists and photographers use visual presentation to create an impact on the world around them. Nine Fire people have an irrepressible energy and make great actors, performers and politicians. Keeping a balance between the inner need for expression and support is vital for Fire personalities. Fire people stand out and need the Wood element and personalities for support. Fire people need to feel secure and maintain a subtle control to sustain professional and personal growth. When balanced they inspire us all.

Earth

22)

MOUNTAIN   TAI CHI   EARTH

BUILDERS AND EARTH

Earth as in Building is solid and strong; it needs to be rooted and dependable.

23) EARTH is located in 3 areas of the Bagua compass. It is grounded, heavy, solid and is represented by the Trigram for MOUNTAIN, (NE) and EARTH (SW) and the YIN YANG symbol (center) which holds all ENERGIES as we live on it and are held by it.

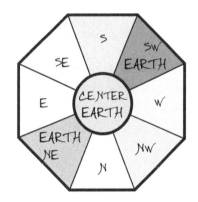

EARTH LIVES IN THE
SW, NE & THE CENTER

EARTH SHAPE

24)

The Earth Element
(Earth is the child of Fire, parent of Metal & the grandparent of Water)

Earth is enduring and giving. Earth, also called soil is both gathering and settling. Embodied by the harvest energy of early fall its energy tends to move downwards. Its expression is feminine, like that of the caregiver, the element that nurtures humanity. Earth has maturity as a theme and honesty as a quality. We are connected to Mother Earth on a primal level. Earth is reliable, steady and ever present. It symbolizes abundance and the grounding beneath us. Earth energy acts as a symbol of the Heart Space; the heart of a building or land mass in Feng Shui. The Earth Element is allocated to the last twenty days of each season as the transitional period between them. The element EARTH holds 3 locations of the 9 areas on the Bagua. In the SW its Trigram is KUN for Earth and is three broken Yin lines; the ultimate feminine. In the NE its Trigram is KEN for Mountain and is two broken Yin lines under a solid Yang line; a masculine expression. Earth takes the center spot and is androgynous or both yin and yang. It does not have a Trigram so its symbol is Tai Chi or the Yin/Yang symbol. Earth forms a band of energy from SW, Center and NE on the Bagua.

In Design : In the home Earth shows as low, heavy pieces of furniture. It has the most variety of colors of all elements encompassing the colors of fall. These range from yellows, browns, oranges and pinks; and all tones we know as earth tones, including off white, beige and taupe. Terra cotta and ceramics are earth and symbolize it in a creative way. Square shapes or low rectangles are the prominent Earth shapes.

In the landscape the type of mountains that are earth will be those that are grouped together or presenting as solid, continuous, even shapes in nature.

Builders make things to last. They know about structure and the creative process through application. Good buildings are grounded in the earth. Foundations, built into earth are how builders manifest a design. Builders get things done and personify Earth through their work. Meticulous, steady and methodical, builders are the nurturers of ideals which lay at the core of this element.

Human Characteristics : People who have Earth characteristics have either number 2, 5 or 8 as their Nine Star Ki Principle numbers. All three personalities are generally highly functional and practical. Generally earth types are generous and nurturing, solid and reliable. Conservative by nature they present things in an unbiased way. Naturally intuitive and dependable they are often called upon to assist others. When they give too much they can become unbalanced and ungrounded. They can then become over dependent on those around them instead of being the ones we depend on. Earth people have healthy constitutions, yet it will be the stomach that is weakened when they are under pressure or stress. Earth types need to be appreciated otherwise they become weak and diminished. Trusting gut feelings is a powerful antidote for these personalities. They are very effective as planners, administrators and organizers. They excel in farming, real estate, mining, landscaping, recycling, and do well as environmentalists. Basic to Earth types is building the relationships and the overseeing of details. Earth types must learn to nurture self as well as others to move forward and flourish both personally and professionally.

Metal

HEAVEN

LAKE

DEVELOPERS AND METAL

Metal as in Development is direct, solid and concise. It is creative and compliant with a definitive result as a completion point.

26) Metal is located in 2 areas of the Bagua compass. It is malleable, alchemic, glittery and is represented by the Trigram for HEAVEN (NW) and LAKE (W). Its holds the energy of late harvest and fall and is replenishing and pleasurable.

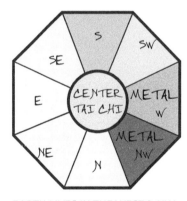

EARTH LIVES IN THE WEST & NW

METAL SHAPE

The Metal Element
(Metal is the child of Earth, the parent of Water & grandparent of Wood)

Metal's nature embodies movement that is both inward and solidifying. Metal energy moves towards completion and starts again. It is an enduring force and one of constant change. The controlling nature of Metal is due to its need to move from a liquid to a solid state. Metal is linked with money and currency, traditionally measured in gold and silver. Its metaphor is that of cash flow (liquid state) which actualizes as currency (solid state). Metal's strength is in its flexibility and creativity which yields substantial results. Metal is associated with the Late Autumn and the enjoyment of the harvest period. It takes up the two areas of the Bagua that symbolize descending Yang energy and ascending Yin energy. In the West it is the Trigram TUI meaning Lake which has two solid Yang lines below a broken Yin line, making it feminine. In the NW is the Trigram CHIEN meaning Heaven. These three solid Yang lines represent the ultimate masculine. Metal is not easily changed when rigid yet when used to conduct a current shows a dualistic nature. It is linked to communications and electronics as a conduit for information. Twenty first century technology with fiber optics has given us the worldwide web; an example of Metals' creative and functional use. The persevering quality of metal is its diversity and alchemic nature, allowing it to conduct ideas and thoughts and turn base elements to gold.

In Design The colors of metal are associated with autumn. The golden colors of early fall eventually change to white and silver in the landscape. Metal symbology appears in design as archways and spiral shapes. Its dualism shows in its softer, circular manifestation opposing its linear, sharp and pointed forms. Metal appears as appliances, metal accessories, metal beds, stainless steel and various house hold items. Modern architecture presents Metal as structural and strong.

In the Landscape We see Metal in singular or clumps of mountains with rounded tops; exuding feminine shapes. The landforms in China and southern Thailand are good examples.

Development is a substantial forward movement. Developers need good communication and flow of information to shape their vision. Multitasking moves towards a singular outcome, like liquid moving into a solid state. The process has a masculine edge with a feminine creative aspect. Their razor sharp abilities pull together ideas that manifest in solid results and completion. Moving from the rigidity of control to flexibility and fluidity allows developers to find balance.

Human Characteristics People who have #6 Metal and #7 Metal as their principle Nine Star Ki Numbers are strong and resolute in their expression of individuality. Metal is connected to the organs, lungs, skin and colon, which are the moderators of change. The challenge for metal types is that they do have difficulty with change in their lives. Depending on other aspects of personality this can create a need for control and an inability to shift opinions easily, Metal people are strong, ambitious and independent by nature. Channellers of ideas and transformation. Metal people can be rigid and strong yet flexible. In the fields of computer hardware, mechanics, money investment and market traders, transportation and surgery work with aspects of Metal. When metal presents as a problematic, exploring new options is the antidote. Learning to let go of control and of what does not serve, allows Metal types balance and grow, both personally and professionally.

Water

WATER

WATER AND DESIGNERS

Water as in Design is a deep and thoughtful process of integrating information. The results allow the best expression of a look, a feeling and a solution to given criteria.

28) WATER is located in one area only of the Bagua compass. It is organic, deep, moving and is represented by the Trigram for WATER (N)

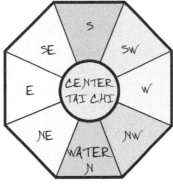

WATER LIVES IN THE NORTH ONLY

WATER SHAPE

29)

The Water Element

(Water is the Parent of Wood and the Child of Metal and the grandparent of Fire)

Water energy is a combination of fluidity and stillness. It is penetrating and floating. Deep water can easily change to the fast, bubbly movement of a stream. Water is present in many forms: the depths of the ocean, the rapid flowing river or the stillness of a pond. Water shape shifts from ice to liquid, steam and mist, giving it a mysterious nature. Water's multidimensionality and Fire's brilliance make them the two most powerful of the five elements, each taking up a single location on the Bagua. Water is located in the North and its Trigram KAN has two yin lines holding the one yang line, making it dominantly Yang. Just as north and winter are about regenerative power, Water has the ability to transform and rebirth. Water is ever present and necessary in our lives, and symbolizes deep internal wisdom. Its metaphor alludes to reaching for the depths to find answers. It teaches us the quality of deepening connections with our true selves as its influence can create lasting change.

In Design Water alludes to a deep and introspective process. Good design is about finding solutions that are felt as much as seen. Water symbolism is seen in design and the environment as aquariums, fountains, water taps and even the simple garden hose. It appears as organic shapes, such as waves and abstract art. The colors are blue and black and the particularly cool tone, blue purple. Water can be symbolically created in design by way of dry creek beds, Zen gardens, photographs of water and organic sculptures. Dry water features must be made active through intention and placement while actual water features are more potent. Using asymmetry in design can create balance in an environment and reflects waters random, fluid nature.

In the Landscape Water shaped Mountains will appear wavy and undulating. Their organic shapes embody many features simultaneously.

Designers Designers, like the element Water, must be in a constant flow and embody its many forms to find solutions in challenging situations. Designers explore all aspects of human nature with thoughtfulness. A good design reflects both the physical and psychological aspects that shape our world.

Human Characteristics and other Professions People who have their principle number as # 1 Water can be excellent communicators. They have the potential to tune into deeper emotions and express them. Water personalities are as diverse as water itself. These folk can be like a babbling brook, fast moving river, soft steam, or allusive like mist or rain. Many water personalities are adept in their abilities to move through issues easier than others. Water has both an adventurous nature when flowing but can stagnate when it is blocked. Water is naturally fluid which allows these folks to go with the flow. Care must be taken not to get caught up in others' plans as it is harder for Water types to back out. An imbalanced Water person will be inconsistent and docile, depending excessively on others or appearing aloof and shut down. This can create self sabotage: emotionally, psychically and physically. Water types are vulnerable to cold and damp and need a lot of sleep. Water is manifest in researchers, importers, exporters, personnel department heads and in those in the medical professions. Obvious water types are firefighters and fisherman. They have strength and internal knowing. They go to the depths to find answers that elude others. Their affinity to both the concrete and abstract give them professional and personal strength.

Wood

THUNDER

WIND

DECORATORS AND WOOD

Wood is movement and direction. It is felt, noticed and often predictable.

WOOD is located in 2 areas of the Bagua compass. It is fast moving, energized, irrepressible and is represented by the Trigram for THUNDER (E) and WIND (SE).

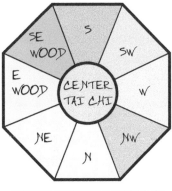

WOOD LIVES IN THE EAST & SE

WOOD SHAPE

The Wood Element

(Wood is the child of Water, parent of Fire & the grandparent of Earth)

Wood is a powerful Yang energy. It cannot be held back as it embodies the joy and transformation of birthing. Wood energy symbolizes fresh and optimistic outlooks. Wood is growth, its season is springtime and its time of day is morning. Wood arouses us out of our sleepiness and awakens and refreshes our energy. Wood can be unpredictable and wild or it can be very consistent and fruitful. Wood symbolizes new beginnings, new projects, and going in new directions. The two areas of the Bagua devoted to the wood element are SE & E. In the East it is the Trigram ZHEN meaning Thunder; represented by two Yin broken lines held up by one solid Yang line, making it Yang. SE is the Trigram XUN meaning Wind; represented by two broken yin lines on top held up by a solid Yang line, giving it a Yang Nature. Wood energy brings the power of the past into view. It is also about taking the fortunate blessings of the present forwards into possibilities for the future.

In design Wood in the decor is what makes an impression with style, color and overall look. A good design offers a base upon which the decorative aspects are built. In interiors wood is symbolized by wood itself yet is also seen as tall objects due to the direction and movement being tree like. Decorative aspects that inspire upward movement embody Wood symbology. All shades of green, from the lime tones to deep emeralds and even blue greens are considered Wood colors. Although Wood grows in the earth, browns are not considered Wood tones.

In the landscape Wood is symbolized by height and shape reflecting a tree's ability to reach upwards. It not only appears in wood furniture and building materials but also in tall, sculptural pieces. Log and timber frame homes symbolize Wood and Earth as they are heavy and grounded.

Decorators Decoration evokes a message, sensibility and emotion. The wood element suits decorators due to their inspired and meticulous attention to detail. The visual affect of good decor seeks to uplift our spirits; true to woods nature. Embellishment of a good design reflects these wood qualities.

Human Characteristics : People with Nine Star Ki # 3 and # 4 Wood as principle numbers, exhibit a very active nature. They have moralistic tendencies, setting high standards for themselves and others. They are self-confident and motivated. Expansive in nature, Wood types can be involved in many fields. They are social and cooperative, rather than solitary like metal or water. Financial security is second nature to them as they are confident in their abilities. Imbalance occurs only when they take on too much at once. Wood personalities can then lose focus, going from one project to another, without the ability to complete any. Multitasking within one task only, allows them to focus and not scatter energy unnecessarily. Professions such as astrology, animation, invention or life coaching or spiritually expressive careers such as preachers, spiritual leaders and counsellors symbolize the Wood element. These folks can see beyond the norm and bring innovation to the interpretation of these professions. Other obvious professions are wood workers and those in paper products. Wood types are both influential and easily influenced. They must take care to discern others' intentions as they are very vulnerable. Balancing this weakness with their ability to be influential allows them deep personal and professional growth.

In Summary

Relating these five design disciplines to each of the 5 elements deepens our understanding of core characteristics within the human dimension. *The Elements and Who We Are, page 10 and 11,* asks questions that decode how each profession or livelihood exhibits elemental characteristics that reflect our placement in the whole. The impulse behind career choices broadens our relationship and understanding of planetary energies. Recognizing how the elements are part of everything, leads to balancing environments that we inhabit or create. Whether visualizing, developing, designing, building or embellishing spaces, this knowledge will change your relationships to what you do. Feng Shui allows those in the design and development professions to select optimal aspects for all applications. Whether it be for buildings, homes, monuments or the enhancement of sacred sites, the process of elemental awakening becomes a part of us. The Schools of Feng Shui will offer the context for further integration.

Each of the elements are allotted one of the four seasons. Earth is given the 20 day period at the end of each season as a transition time; from one season to another. Each element is given a cardinal direction with the Earth assigned to the center and as such ties all the others together.

The Elements present during the year of the client's birth, Including Nine Star Ki information can give a Feng Shui consultant valuable insights. Knowing a clients elements, especially what is missing, is fundamental in balancing an environment for them personally. When there are multiple persons sharing a space, charts are combined to look at what is required individually and as a group. Elemental balance can be achieved with color, furnishings, symbolism and placement. Individual spaces are considered as are shared spaces.

Enhancing balance and harmony with elemental knowledge takes design to another level. Combining this information with a client's directional energy and Bagua placement is how Feng Shui Design can microsite issues and assist clients rectify them. The elements can play a huge role in the process.

THE SCHOOLS of FENG SHUI

COMPASS SCHOOL, FORM SHCOOL and INTUITIVE FENG SHUI

I personally started my practice as an intuitive Feng Shui consultant who had read one book. In the Introduction the 'Being personally activated' I share what led me to formal training. It would have been beneficial to have more insight into the applications of the various schools of Feng Shui, their nuances and differences during my first seven years of study. This section seeks to clarify the various ways to apply Feng Shui theory and guide readers towards publications that reflect a personal style which will enhance your life and profession.

There are many ways of interpreting Feng Shui. Each consultant will have a particular way of practicing a methodology. In the West, practitioners have to choose whether to follow ancient Asian style or Feng Shui that has been adapted for western use. Intuitive Feng Shui, which lay outside both of these ideals, is one's inner knowing about placement, flow and health. It is the intuitive that attracts us to the Art of Feng Shui.

TRADITIONAL COMPASS SCHOOL

What we know as Traditional Compass School was developed in China where the visible landscape did not indicate obvious energy flow. In areas where land forms were minimal, people tuned into the wind directions/Feng and the water ways/Shui as reference points. This led to the observation of electromagnetic and geomantic earth energies as guides to understand the environment. Invented in China, the compass gave birth to Compass School Feng Shui. In modern Feng Shui practice, as in the past, the compass is used to find actual directions. The Feng Shui Compass or Bauga is what is used primarily in Western Feng Shui Practice. The Bagua referred to in this text and most Feng Shui publications is a simplified version of the Traditional Lopan, the compass-like instrument used by Feng Shui Masters. Bagua information is transposed over land or a structure to inform us what energies lie where. An example: A south facing entry will have full sun exposure making it a lively, active area. Vision and Fame are the energies associated with the element Fire and the direction South. Reading a compass gives a practitioner a feel for the tone of a home based on direction. It is the observation of natural phenomena which reflects a Taoist perspective.

TRADITIONAL COMPASS SCHOOL FENG SHUI

is historically what Asian Masters use. The Lopan is used to gather a wide spectrum of information about a location for a specific consultation. Authors of Traditional Feng Shui ideology are of Asian descent or have studied with traditional Asian masters and practitioners.

Feng Shui in the West has evolved from aspects of both Traditional Compass School and Form School. The difference is that Traditional Compass School can become a very involved investigation. As it adheres to the use of exact compass directions to read energy, the depth of information on an Asian Lopan is very mathematically complex. It also uses aspects of Form School. Traditional Compass School often surpasses most Western understanding in its depth and detail.

Traditional Compass School also uses both Landscape Feng Shui and Form School ideologies. As an all encompassing practice, each level provides insights that lay at the root of Feng Shui investigations. Each Feng Shui practitioner will apply the Bagua according to the school, or master that guides them. Publications on Feng Shui do not often clarify the subtle differences, so to those practicing Feng Shui without formal training, this can be very confusing. Whether it be Black Hat, Form, Landscape or Traditional Compass, know that all have relevance and are related. The traditional Lopan, as mentioned above is very detailed and beyond most Western practitioners and clients. Therefore using the Bagua will depend on what school or ideology appeals to you. This text seeks to differentiate and guide readers to this conclusion.

Vernacular Southwest architecture blends into the landscape, exuding harmony and tranquility within the environment.

FORM SCHOOL FENG SHUI

Form School is based on what surrounds us from the microcosm to the macrocosm. It begins with the observation of our immediate environment; whether it be within a room, a building or in the near and far landscape. Landscapes are powerful reference points. The way a location feels dictates how we experience it. From this perspective Compass information may take a secondary role. The Difference is that Form School does not take the Compass directions into account in a literal way.

The Compass School has not been given priority in North America. A portion of the population is hardwired to directional energy. For people who love maps and never get lost the compass is hard to ignore. People who are dyslexic or challenged by maps and following verbal instruction, find the compass a huge challenge. Knowing which category you fall in will determine which School of Feng Shui will work best for you. Traditional Asian Masters who have come to the West have had the challenge of teaching and practicing a complex art. Often from a western perspective it comes across as secretive due to its intricacy. Asian clients put ultimate trust in the learned Grand Masters. Understanding what is being done is not as much a concern as a belief in the results; a trust that is deeply cultural. Practicing Feng Shui in the West would have to evolve for the information to hit the mainstream. The history of its evolution on the West Coast of North America is a fascinating story.

Form School In Western Culture:

Black Hat Sect

In North America in the late 60's a Chinese master by the name of Master Thomas Lin Yun came to Berkley, California and started to teach Feng Shui. He called his school The Black Hat Sect of Tibetan Buddhist Feng Shui. Of the 4 distinct sects of Tibetan Buddhism the Bon sect is the most mystical. Although it uses aspects of Feng Shui it would not reflect what we as North Americans, Europeans or Latin Americans would recognize as Modern Feng Shui for home and business . A large part of The Black Hat Sect of Tibetan Buddhist Feng Shui application is rooted in spiritual practice. The syllabus of Master Lin's school focuses as much on meditation and spiritual practice as Feng Shui knowledge. Why is this? To his credit Master Lin Yun simplified the study of Feng Shui by eliminating certain aspects of the Traditional Compass school; specifically the exact reading of compass directions.

Instead, Master Lin Yun created a totally new school known as The Black Hat Sect. He did this by using important parts of the Traditional practice: The Form School and the 3 Door System. Combined with a deep and ancient spirituality of the Bon Sect of Tibetan Buddhism it formed an ideology that could be applied in the West. His arrival in California in the sixties was timely. A cultural and sexual revolution was brewing throughout the USA. Anti-Vietnam war demonstrations and racial division in the southern states were contentious issues. Many were looking for alternatives to the status quo. When Master Lin Yun arrived in the San Francisco Bay area, minds were open to Asian Pacific alternative ideologies. Traditional Chinese Medicine, Tai Chi, Zen Meditation, Buddhist philosophies and Feng Shui were captivating concepts. Master Lin Yun's teachings focused primarily on Form School not Compass School. A component or layer of the Traditional Feng Shui called the 3 Door System was employed which dictated how the compass would be used.

In this System which falls under Form School ideology indicates that NORTH is always located at the front door or the side of the building where the front door is located. This component of Feng Shui application is referred to as the '3 Door System' which originates from traditional practice. The Front door will be located on the right, center, or left. Eliminating the compass simplified its application.

BUDDHISM IN FENG SHUI

The spiritual aspect of Buddhism that Master Lin Yun introduced to the study of Feng Shui created a concentrated practice which served to focus one's intention. If one is not using a compass, then prayerful intention becomes a means of activation. If not following the energy that an actual direction has, there needs to be both thoughtful prayer and visual reminders. The 3 Door System serves to create a spacial awareness to hold Feng Shui Cures or adjustments. The use of visual reminders such as mirrors, crystals, flutes, and other cures are essential. North American response to these physical reminders did not help with a belief in the superstitious nature of Feng Shui. In essence, practicing the Black Hat Sect takes much dedication, prayer and reactivation of cures or adjustments to maintain balance in a space. This is why the use of Black Hat School of Feng Shui does not work for everyone as there are constant activations and cures to maintain. The use of the compass is more in tune with the natural earth cycles and energy flow.

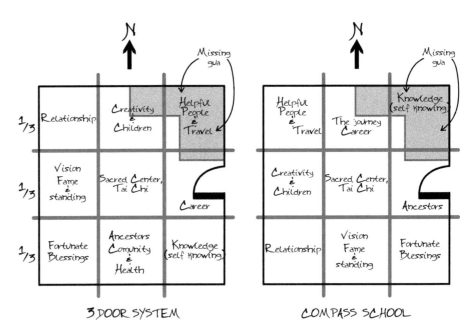

As a traditional practitioner, I use the Compass School primarily to place the Bagua, but I also double check my findings by using the 3 Door System. I use the Compass Information as 80% and the 3 Door System as 20% of my findings. It acts as the backup reference. If the actual front door is due North on the compass both schools of thought and methodologies are synchronized.

There are cases where these percentages are changed as each application and client differ. The purpose of using both is to discover the underlying or subliminal energies affecting a challenged location.

When the Form School of Feng Shui is followed, North is always placed on the side where the main door faces. Normally doors occur in one of 3 areas.

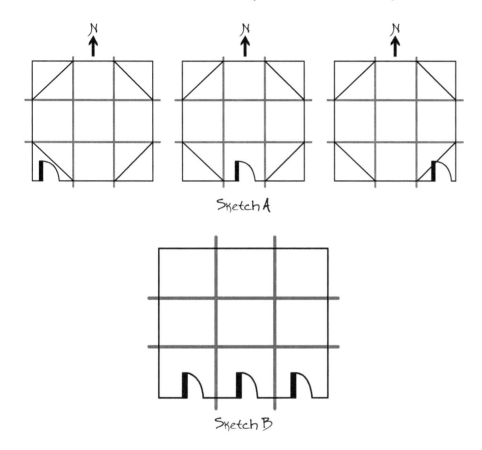

Sketch A

Sketch B

Sketch A shows three homes with doors in one of each area, where a door could be located on the 'face' of a building. No matter the actual direction the 3 Door System will call this facing side NORTH. Thus the entry will be in one of three Guas.

Sketch B shows these possibilities on one sketch and an illustration common to show the 3 door system. In the 3 Door System this means that the door will enter into Knowledge/NE, Career/N or Helpful People/Travel/NW.

The task of introducing Feng Shui Knowledge to North America was a vast and ambitious undertaking. Teaching North Americans the basis of Compass School when so many are directionally challenged was an approach that did not always work well. Master Lin Yun's use of the Tibetan practices of the Bon Sect and his simplification of directional understanding by using the 3 Door System as a base was brilliant.

Over the last 45 years many have studied the Black Hat School and through books and teachings it has become a standard Western practice. When there is reference to Master Thomas Lin Yun or to the Black Hat, know that you are reading a hybrid version of the ancient art of Feng Shui.

In personal studies and teaching over the years I have expanded and shared my personal knowledge of the Black Hat, Traditional Compass School, Geomancy and Energy Clearing. I expected clients and students to be confused at times and to question which school or methodology to use. Ultimately this is a personal choice. In reality, the Lopan is not used in depth in the West as more clients cannot grasp its many intricate layers, and are not willing to invest in something they do not understand. Having studied the Lopan I find few specific clients wanting to go into its depths. Master Lin Yun's methodology worked in getting Feng Shui recognized in the West. All books written by his students are recognizable as Black Hat Sect.

The SCHOOLS of FENG SHUI have a direct relevance to Design application especially when it comes to entrance ways. Entrances shape our first impressions; whether it be to a piece of land, a building or individual spaces. In Section Three there is an in depth look at entrance ways in design. Understanding the different ideologies and schools of Feng Shui can be instrumental in interpreting entrances. Linked to Career and one's journey through life, and referenced in all schools of Feng Shui, entrance ways are core to the study of Feng Shui and Design.

FORM SCHOOL FENG SHUI is linked to Landscape as it incorporates the study of the actual forms in the environment which coincide with the 5 elements. It is the form in the landscape that dictates the natural entrance to a geographical area. In Ancient applications the form was dictated by mountains, valleys and water ways.

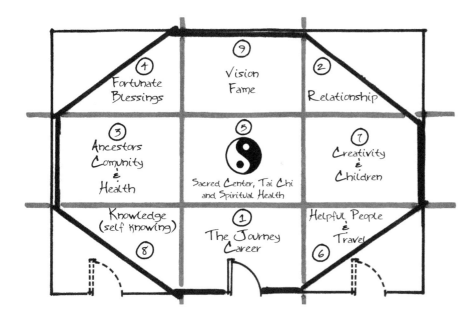

Bagua placement will stretch to fit a home or building.

The prevailing winds and sun's path determines how land or forms in the landscape are interpreted. Human development follows what nature dictates thus valleys and waterways gave way to the locations where people were able to build, farm, fish and live. Nomadic cultures paid special attention to what forms surrounded their camps for gathering resources and protection.

These basic principles have been alive in all evolving cultures. Landscape Feng Shui can exist apart from the Form School, but Form School cannot be applied without consideration of Landscape Feng Shui. It is through understanding the elements and animals that we can check if there is balance. Body Landscape refers to the human form and how it is placed to allow optimal functioning of the immune system. Our homes, buildings and communities are an extension of the human form and as such serves as a reference point in all environments.

BODY LANDSCAPE

Feng Shui Visualization

Take a few minutes to visualize your body landscape. Start in a standing position with back straight, eyes relaxed and looking forward. Concentrate on the front of the body and how it interacts with the environment around us. Concentrate first on the front of the body, this is where the sense of sight informs us. When blocked we cannot see where we are going. Then concentrate on the back; the area of the body vulnerable to what it cannot see. When standing against a wall or tree we have good backing. Next concentrate the right side and then the left. Hearing is related to both sides. Then feel the core of your being. A good focal point is a few inches below the navel. This is a power spot, known as the Tantien or Hara from which we assimilate information from all the senses and directions. Now extend your left arm up and think of the sunrise in that direction as the start of a cycle. You are ready to delve into the world of Landscape Feng Shui.

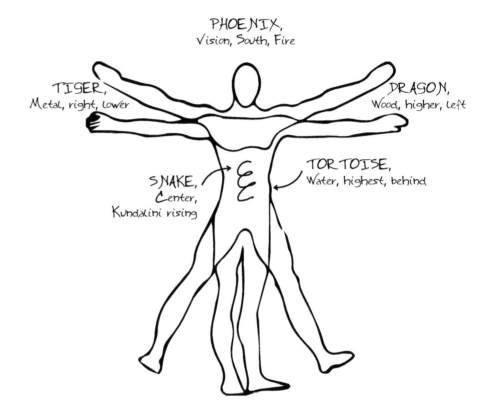

Landscape Feng Shui and the Human Form

Landscape Feng Shui

Landscape Feng Shui is a fundamental building block in understanding placement. It begins with the human form, which like plants, seek the sun for warmth and energy. It is natural to stand facing the sun which is typically South. In diagrams of the Bagua or Feng Shui compass, South will always be situated at the top, not on the bottom as we see in map orientation. This is in direct relation to how the human body naturally looks up to face the sun.

A large percentage of human sustenance enters our mouths as food and liquids. The front of the body is very interactive with our environment through the senses of sight, taste and smell. The Feng Shui orientation towards the sun and South aligns to the element Fire. In cycles of time we relate South to noon and to summer in the northern hemisphere. Information gathering by way of the senses, is actively dynamic at the front of the body. This area is Yang in nature and is symbolized by the PHOENIX. This powerful bird wants a clear view and no obstacles so it can take off and soar.

Opposite our front is our back which is unseen, often forgotten or ignored. The dark side of the body is related to the direction North and is aligned to the element Water. In cycles of time it relates to midnight and winter. The back is the location of the spine in the skeletal system or what supports us. Having good backing in life is important and our backs amplify this metaphor in Landscape Feng Shui. The back symbolizes what is hidden from view thus is considered Yin. The sense of touch is more acute in this vulnerable area. Our spinal system houses nerve endings and important meridians which are crucial to health and well-being. The TORTOISE is the animal associated with North. With its hard protective shell it represents strength and durability against attack.

With the front body facing South the left is considered East. It is the masculine side that aligns with left brain activity in human physiology. Behaviourally the left brain controls the activity of the opposite and right side. It explains why many people are right handed as it's the leading side.

The East, the energy of spring and morning aligns with the element Wood. As greenery and new growth unfolds around us, we are pulled into the magic of new beginnings. This rising, unstoppable Yang force is represented by the DRAGON. Dragon energy embodies the power of spring, the rising sun and growth. Dragon will rise up to fight if threatened.

The left side of the body relates to the West. It is the feminine side of the brain. The left side of the body is related to late afternoon, the fall season and aligns with the element Metal. It is the harvest time, both abundant and nurturing. This is aligned with the feminine and Yin in nature. In the fall we turn inward in preparation for winter. It is calmer, quieter and softer than spring and summer dynamics. A powerful time in itself, it is represented by TIGER. Tiger energy is close to the ground, stealthy and protective. The female Tiger moves in close to the family to protect it should there be danger. The fifth direction or container for all directions and energies lies at the center. The center is therefore associated with the element Earth, our source of sustenance. Crucial to our well- being, it provides nurturing both on a physical and spiritual level. Earth sits at the center holding in it a portion of each of all the other elements yet is one unto itself. Earth is considered the transition times between the seasons or the last 20 days of each season. Physically, it is the pathway up the spine which carries all the fluids and receptors. In the Eastern/ Indian the spine is the Kundalini pathway at the core of the body. Earth is symbolized by the SNAKE,

coiled and taking its cues from all 4 animals surrounding it. Peaceful by nature, the Snake holds its own; it only strikes out when threatened.

The microcosmic placement of the Five Elements on the human body relates directly to the 5 Transformations both physically and personally. The Macrocosm takes us outwards step by step from the body to all the spaces we occupy. This encompasses work areas, homes, buildings, immediate landscapes and the overall environment. Both the macrositing and micrositing of the elements is what Landscape Feng Shui teaches.

The human form is Feng Shui in essence; Feng/ Wind or Breath & Shui/ Water or Substance. How and where we place ourselves has a direct affect on how we experience our world. Experiencing our placement through these lenses touches on the many aspects of the human condition. As humans in a physical form we have control over this experience. With Feng Shui understanding and practice we can also influence what happens in our lives. These teachings are but another perspective to assist our evolution into more conscious beings.

Water flowing gently in a landscape provides flow, harmony and a sense of wonder.

Natural earth formations are an anchor for Landscape Feng Shui.

5 Animals, 5 Directions and 5 Elements,

Any space becomes an extension of the body. Body Landscape takes us from the personal experience to a larger perspective.

Feng Shui Design is about investigating, not just an environment, but those who will occupy it. Creating balance depends on many factors. Elements missing from an individual's birth chart need to show in a home or office for a space to be good for that person. Color, furnishings and spacial arrangement can play an important part in how balance is achieved. In Feng Shui Design the energy is created visually or by symbology.

SHAPES IN THE LANDSCAPE

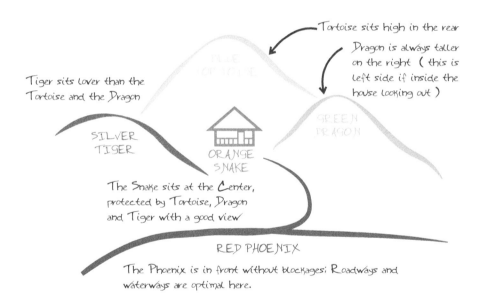

Tortoise sits high in the rear

Dragon is always taller on the right (this is left side if inside the house looking out)

Tiger sits lower than the Tortoise and the Dragon

BLUE TORTOISE

GREEN DRAGON

SILVER TIGER

ORANGE SNAKE

The Snake sits at the Center, protected by Tortoise, Dragon and Tiger with a good view

RED PHOENIX

The Phoenix is in front without blockages; Roadways and waterways are optimal here.

In Landscape Feng Shui the elements take on a new dimension when paired with the 5 Animals that represent them. The elemental relationship to the Body Landscape broadens into the actual landscape.

Microcosm to Macrocosim

The Center of a home is the #5 Earth section or Tai Chi, its spiritual center. This will be the same for Compass or Form as the center does not change with direction. In this spiritual center or Tai Chi it is important for the energy to move easily and pool. Avoid designs that have stairwells, bathrooms or fireplaces in the Tai Chi. Energy moving too fast here may affect the Spiritual Health and well being of occupants.

Moving from the microcosm to the macrocosm this same philosophy can be applied to land development. The center is often the best location for a home or building placement so geophysical or other disturbances here are not optimal.

Important to note:

When developing land it is crucial to know how geophysically active the Tai Chi area is. This includes fault and water lines, and underground pooling water sources. Metaphysical influences such as burial sites, ceremonial sites and human memory imprints can also affect the Sacred Center/Tai Chi of a piece of land. This applies to the 3 Door System, Traditional Compass School and Form School. When the Tai Chi of land is disturbed or too active, the land may never feel comfortable for occupants causing developments to fail. Power spots on the planet have energies that people visit for short periods to feel the impact of subterranean sources, but human occupancy in these areas is highly unlikely.

The TORTOISE sits in the NORTH

The Tortoise is an ancient symbol in many cultures. It carries its home on its back and is very self contained. Placing the Tortoise at our backs symbolizes support. The concept of the spine being the core support for the body is related in our physical landscape as the back. This strength is behind the expression "Ive got your back". The spine is the unseen part of the human body, the form through which the nervous system, specific meridians and blood vessels pass. The rib cage, with its strength at the back, supports all the internal organs. The Tortoise speaks to the hidden and mysterious energies of the divine feminine and the Water element. In Landscape Feng Shui the Tortoise is assigned the highest point, or mountain to the rear of home or building. It is also assigned a solid wall for the Body Landscape. This strength behind us protects us from what we cannot see.

The TORTOISE embodies
- YIN
- NORTH
- WINTER
- MIDNIGHT
- The WATER ELEMENT
- The COLORS: BLUE, BLACK and BLUE PURPLE (cool purple)
- The ENERGY; deep mysterious, thoughtful, sensitive & hidden

The DRAGON sits in the EAST

Moving clockwise directionally we visit the left side of the body. In Landscape Feng Shui this is the East. The left side of the brain is considered male or the masculine expression. The East embodies the yang energy of the rising sun. This is an active, often aggressive energy which awakens us to be in the world and participate. We place the Dragon in the East as it embodies the powerful dynamic that is revered throughout Asian cultures. The Dragon's ability to fly and wield fire makes it a fierce protector. Dragon mythology inspires awe and greatness. This is also the direction of the Wood element, which is a rising energy as is the sun in the East. Wood symbols are trees, tall mountains, high walls and tall furniture. In Landscape Feng Shui items to the left should be higher in stature than items placed on the right side or Tiger side.

The DRAGON embodies
- YANG
- EAST
- SPRING
- EARLY MORNING
- The ELEMENT WOOD
- The COLORS GREEN; LIME to EMERALD and all shades in between
- The ENERGY; uplifting, forward moving, dynamic and relentless

The PHOENIX sits in the SOUTH

Next in progression from the East, we follow the sun's movement in the sky towards its apex; high noon or mid summer. This is the culmination of the rising yang energy and is where the Phoenix takes flight. The Phoenix is a mythical animal who rises from its own ashes to move towards a greater destiny. This is the area in front of the body in Landscape Feng Shui. All winged creatures and aircraft need space and a clear view in front to take off. The front of the body is where we take in the exterior world through our senses, so it's important to see clearly and be focused. The metaphor and symbology is that we need to see where we are going to move forward and actualize our destiny, dreams and visions. When there is clarity of vision we will reach our destinations. Physical obstructions, whether architectural or natural that block the Phoenix can hold us back from our goals. Described in terms and concepts under Ming Tang, what we see is vital to the placement of buildings and homes within an environment. The Phoenix is always in the front.

The PHOENIX embodies
- YANG
- SOUTH
- SUMMER
- MID DAY
- The FIRE ELEMENT
- The COLORS: RED and RED PURPLE (warm purple)
- The ENERGY; Vision, actualizing goals, clarity, truth and brilliance

The TIGER sits in the WEST

After the peak energy of Fire there is a shift into a quiet, slower pace. The move from South towards SW and West is when Yang shifts to Yin. The animal here is TIGER and it represents an inward movement with its powerful, assuring presence. Unlike the Dragon of the East, the Tiger moves with a slower intention. TIGER represents the Metal element which when it goes from liquid to solid, contracts. Tiger represents both the early harvest of abundance and gathering and the late fall when leaves are gone from the trees. It shows on the right side of the body which is feminine. The feminine Yin energy goes inward, opposite to that of the masculine which moves upward. The phrase 'crouching tiger' is a metaphor in Feng Shui design for the placement of lower physical objects on our right sides. Tiger, on the right, is lower and viewed as smaller land formations. Inside it would be walls with windows and low furnishings at the right hand side of a room. It is always viewed from the location that provides good backing and optimal Ming Tang or view.

The TIGER embodies
- YIN
- WEST
- AFTERNOON TO EVENING
- FALL
- HARVEST
- The METAL ELEMENT
- The COLORS: WHITE, GOLD and SILVER: at times BRONZE and PASTELS
- ENERGY; Gathering, quieting, enjoyment, relaxation & solidification.

The SNAKE sits at the CENTER

The culmination of all energies sits at the center with the SNAKE. The Snake is a powerful symbol of the Kundalini that rises up through the center of the spine. The Snake is coiled, poised and at rest. It is alert to what happens around it taking its cues from the other four animals. There is a spiritual aspect to this location, as it is a bridge from the heavens to the earth. Man stands connected to the ground with arms outstretched, holding space between heaven and earth, acting as a conduit between the two. Earth coincides with the center, being both the physical landscape, and our grounding.

As the Earth element is the last 20 days of each season it has a portion of each other element and season within it. The Snake at the center is both protected by and acts as a nucleus for inward and outward movement. Earth encompasses all other energies and radiates spherically, yet it is an element and animal separate from the others. Symbolically it is the heart and center of all other elements. Note that the symbol for health in allopathic medicine is that of two snakes circling each other as in a DNA strand.

The SNAKE Embodies
- YIN and YANG
- THE LAST 20 DAYS OF EACH SEASON
- UNIFICATION
- SACRED CENTER
- The EARTH ELEMENT
- The COLORS: PINK, ORANGE, BROWN, YELLOW, and TAUPE
- The ENERGY; Union, Sharing, Coming Together, Androgyny, Spirituality

Although largely symbolic, these animals are fundamental in understanding Landscape Feng Shui. These concepts are often overlooked by many interested in this practice. It can be confusing when Form School is considered simply Landscape Feng Shui without exploring all its implications. Its understanding can be paramount in the development and design world as we can learn much from going deeper.

The 5 Elements & Landscape Feng Shui in Design

The five elements are applied in the microcosm by the use of Body Landscape and macrocosmically by the use of Landscape Feng Shui. Balance can be achieved on many levels by understanding the symbology of the elements, the animals, the forms, the colors and the shapes associated with each. Landscape Feng Shui is a formula which, when used in design and development creates balance and harmony. It can also be used to determine why spaces may not feel right in spite of aesthetics.

As a tool in the Design and Development professions it takes us from the practical use of colors, shapes and placement into deeper symbolic references. As such, Landscape Feng Shui is a vital aspect in Feng Shui Feng Shui design fusion.

How Landscape is Used and
Measured when applying Compass School

Years into my practice I became fully aware of the importance of Landscape Feng Shui. With the many methodologies used to evaluate Feng Shui it was easy to get lost and sidetracked. Having decided that Compass School and the more Traditional approach worked best for me, Landscape Feng Shui seemed less relevant. Working with the Bagua as a designer made more sense in interior application.

It took time, trial and error to look beyond my interior design roots. I realized that the Form, including the Body Landscape was an essential place to start. It was then that my practice shifted. I discovered that when the landscape was good it contributed to a largely balanced Feng Shui energy. Working with the Bagua became secondary for some time while I reevaluated Landscape and Form Schools' overall importance. Master Lim drove home the point that in certain circumstances Landscape Feng Shui could take precedent over all other Feng Shui theory. With time and practice I was able to integrate all my knowledge for a balanced approach.

Lighting, color and placement in landscape design with the house and fence as backing show us a microcosmic example of Landscape Feng Shui.

THE BAGUA

The three dimensional nature of Landscape Feng Shui shifts a two dimensional concept, the Feng Shui Compass or Bagua. Understanding Landscape is an introduction to the Bagua by way of the five elements. The Five Elemental Theory's relationship to the energetic impulses of each direction on the Bagua is key in Feng Shui study. The eight sided BAGUA illustrates directions, elements and the eight trigrams of the I Ching. The center captures all elements and is represented by the Yin/Yang symbol called the Tai Chi. In total, there are nine areas on a Bagua. Each exterior section or direction of the Bagua represents eight universal principles. For example: The East direction is the Trigram for Thunder. Thunder translates on the Bagua as ancestral energy, community and health. The element is wood and the number is three. East aligns with spring, early morning and new beginnings. Thunder is a yang energy that is awakening; offering new possibilities. Thunder is the voice of the ancestors. It aligns with the importance of our health and our place in community. Every Gua's relationship to each of the universal principles carries a lesson and a teaching. When we examine the Bagua new layers of information are revealed. The Bagua follows and repeats the cycles of time that are universal, revealing a natural, easy flow of ideas and information. The hidden beauty of the Bagua, beyond its logic and science, is this deep symbology. It is not surprising to find that the animals of the Chinese Zodiac are represented on

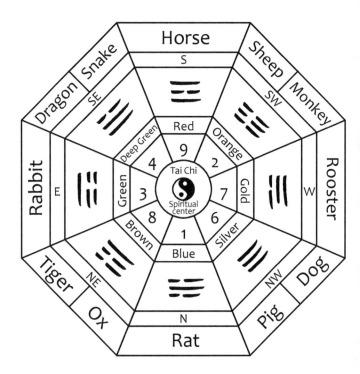

the Bagua. They sit in each direction with the cardinal directions having one animal each and the secondary directions having two animals. For example, the Rabbit is in the East, with ESE the location for the Dragon, and SSE that of the Snake. Each animal aligns with a western astrology sign although this information is not revealed on a Bagua.

The Evolution of the Bagua

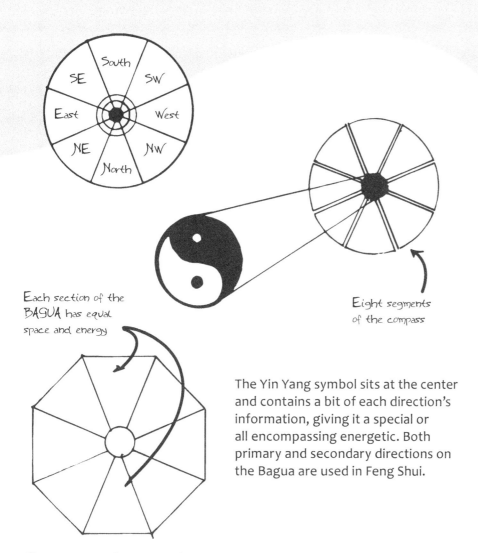

Each section of the BAGUA has equal space and energy

Eight segments of the compass

The Yin Yang symbol sits at the center and contains a bit of each direction's information, giving it a special or all encompassing energetic. Both primary and secondary directions on the Bagua are used in Feng Shui.

The compass was originally created in China in the locations where there was no perceptible forms in the landscape. The discovery and evolution of the compass is thought to be simultaneous to the recognition of landscape Feng Shui. Using forms to read energy became an integrated part of Feng Shui and Geomancy.

Evolution of The Bagua Compass

Reverse Compass

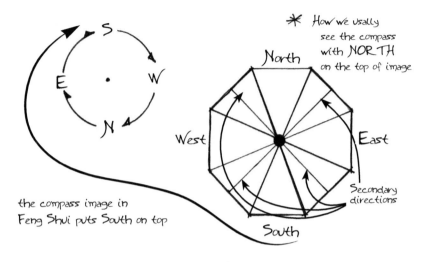

In Feng Shui South is on top, the opposite of what geographical maps show.

Note that South will be found on the top of the Bagua in all reference materials. In cartography, North is oriented at the top of maps. Feng Shui allows the energetic impulse to dictate where information is revealed. South at the top of the Bagua follows the visuals of Fire. Fire, as it relates to the five elements is peak energy. It is mid day, mid summer and the direction South. The Magic Square numbers on the Bagua show the number for Fire, #9, at the top. Fire's symbol is a triangle, with the peak pointing towards the heavens. In Landscape Feng Shui the Phoenix's position is South and like all birds it rises upwards in flight. Humans look up to the Sun as a natural phenomena, so South on top of the Bagua is in a natural, logical position.

Using the Bagua

The Bagua is used in Feng Shui to determine where universal principles and the corresponding concepts are located when placed over land and buildings. The information relates to symbology, elemental energy and the eight directions. The Bagua is used as a tool and primary guide for interpretation of interior and exterior spaces. Every situation is different which is why land, buildings and office spaces are examined and related to its placement, occupants and function.

Compromised areas indicate imbalance. These may be found as irregular land shapes, missing guas, oversized or protruding guas and odd shaped buildings. When applied to design, balance can be built into all basic infrastructure. As an example, a small addition can be favorable or a small missing area can be easily remedied. However, when missing areas or additions are proportionally large, they are more of a challenge to remedy.

The Bagua is as an octagon shape yet it reconfigures into nine equal sections within a square or a rectangle. Each of these nine areas must be equal in size and shape when placed over a space. It can then reveal the concepts and energies in each direction or gua. The Bagua can be macrosited over topographic maps and buildings or microsited over a room or a desk. The Bagua is placed over sites and buildings in one or two ways: according to the Traditional Compass School or Form School/ 3 Door System.

Compass School places the Bauga to align with the actual directions determined by a compass which coincides with those on the Bagua. Form School methodology uses the 3 Door System which allocates North on the Front Door: or the one in which the front door is positioned. The 3 Door System disregards the actual compass directions.

In comprehensive Feng Shui practice, both methods are used. Bagua use is both simple and complex at the same time. Regular shaped buildings and land sites are easier to read. When locations are less uniform in size or oddly shaped, placing the Bagua becomes an art. Skilled Feng Shui consultants will work in accordance to their specific skills and school of study. They will assess anomalies such as the size of missing sections or extensions. Both client and circumstance will dictate the extent of investigations. The Bagua then is as important as reading the forms in the landscape. The Bagua's octagon shape appears in many illustrations throughout the book. Each one exemplifies levels of information and interpretation. A powerful tool, it is used in conjunction with Form School and Landscape Feng Shui knowledge. The relationship of the elements to form and color alone is significant in many professions. As humans we are triggered by color, smell, directional energy and symbolism. In design, as in many walks of life, Bagua knowledge allows us to create, expand and consider new possibilities. Applying the Bagua is both informative and inspirational in every stage of land and building development.

A simple and easy Bagua placement is putting it on a work desk. It is standard to use the 3 Door System locating North, the #1 and Career where one sits at the desk. It symbolizes the entrance to a work area and is a good way to become familiar with the information. Expanding this into a room, building or environment can then be practiced. When one feels confident with the 3 Door System, then Compass School application can be experimented with. Familiarity comes with repetitive use. The information held within the many levels of the Bagua is a process of discovery. It can allow those who use it to transform spaces and make them feel as good as they look. Creating environments that are beautifully enriched leave us with a deep sense of well being.

THE BAGUA: Section by Section

1 WATER and sits in the North. It is both the energy Water and the element Water. The trigram KAN translates as water's flow which relates to passage and JOURNEY through life. The location of the number one symbolizes the starting point which in Feng Shui relates to Career. When in line with our personal Journey, our career will be directly related to our purpose on the planet. The trigram KAN is Yang and represents the middle son in the family.

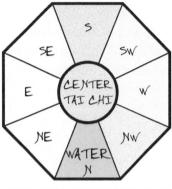

WATER LIVES IN THE NORTH ONLY

#2 is EARTH and sits in the SW. It is both the energy Earth and the element Earth. The trigram is K'UN means earth's ability to provide and nourish. Earth represents the Mother. SW earth energy translates as RELATIONSHIP. It symbolizes the relationship we have to the planet and to each other. Number two indicates a crucial aspect important aspect of life; nurturing and being nurtured. The trigram K'un is feminine and represents the mother.

#3 is THUNDER and sits in the EAST. The trigram is CHEN, the voice of who brought us here. THUNDER translates as our Ancestry, Community and Health. The number three position reminds us of our debt to the ancestors and urges us to move forward with integrity and purpose. This gua symbolizes the formed tree and the Wood element; uplifting, proud and strong. The trigram CHEN is Yang and represents the oldest son.

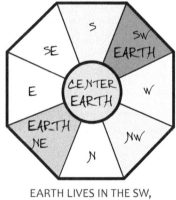

EARTH LIVES IN THE SW,
NE & THE CENTER

#4 is WIND and sits in the SE. The trigram SUN refers to the flow which promotes movement, ideas and growth. The number four encompasses the energy of youth and joy. WIND translates as Abundance and Fortunate Blessings. This gua symbolizes Wood as in the first shoots of grass in

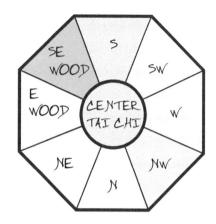

WOOD LIVES IN THE EAST & SE

spring, moving and rejuvenating. The trigram SUN is feminine and represents the oldest daughter.

#5 is called TAI CHI and sits at the center of the Bagua. Considered the Sacred Center as all energies and elements converge here. This central Earth element in its essence holds everything. As the fifth position, it is the portal for the Divine the energy

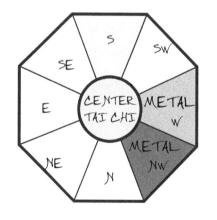

EARTH LIVES IN THE WEST & NW

held between heaven and earth. It symbolizes wholeness. The TAI CHI is androgynous and is referred to the seventh or spiritual child.

#6 is HEAVEN and sits in the NW. The trigram is CHIEN representing the energy of the overseer, the patriarch and responsibility. Heaven translates to that of Helpful People and Travel. Benefactors in our lives allow us movement through life and on the planet. The number six is Metal and personifies this elements solid and impenetrable nature. The trigram CHIEN represents the father and is the ultimate Yang masculine energy.

7 is LAKE and sits in the West. The trigram is TUI and also symbolizes the valley. LAKE translates as Children and Creativity and within it the quality of gratitude. It is the place of rest, relaxation and enjoyment of the beauty in life. The number and position seven is also METAL. This aspect of Metal is softer and more yielding, evolving towards solidification. The trigram TUI is feminine and represents the youngest daughter.

8 is MOUNTAIN and sits in the NE. The Trigram KEN is the masculine location of Earth element. MOUNTAIN translates as Knowledge, both of the outer world and the inner self. Mountain is the eighth position, a place of retreat and contemplation. Mountain represents

endurance and support. As home to volcanic energy it embodies creative, steady action. The trigram Ken represents the youngest son.

9 is FIRE and sits in the South. It embodies both the energy and element Fire. The trigram is LI which translates as one's reputation and community standing. FIRE carries the energy of Vision and Fame which is both visual and compelling. LI embodies passion and allows its expression to move

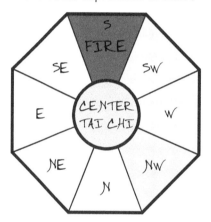

FIRE LIVES IN THE SOUTH ONLY

unconditionally and fully. Fire as an element naturally reaches a peak before burning out. Fire in the ninth position, is a culmination of all that has come before it. Fire burns away all impurities and as a metaphor leaves nothing but the truth. The trigram LI is feminine and represents the middle daughter.

Feng Shui, Metaphor and The Nuances of Chi

Becoming familiar with the different schools of Feng Shui takes time. Landscape Feng Shui is a good starting point to access the overall picture. The Bagua then becomes the most significant tool. Whether using Compass directions or the 3 Door System the goal is to find the locations of specific energies. Symbology and metaphoric analogies are an inherent part of the work, but it will take time to recognize these nuances when using the Bagua and design criteria.

A good example is when Compass School and the 3 Door System match up. When a main door is central and aligns with North, the #1, Water and the Journey or Career, the two schools overlap and the symbolism here is two fold. As well, entrances have a pivotal significance in Feng Shui practice. Number one on the Bagua symbolizes a starting point. Metaphorically, the entrance is associated with our path in life, first impressions and the beginning of a process. Its alignment with Career takes on a deeper significance whether associated with the Bagau or not.

Different forms of Chi

Life Force energy sustains all in the environment. The constant flow of energy/chi can be observed. Sha Chi, Sheng Chi and Si Chi are three Feng Shui terms that differentiate its qualities.

These three terms are useful in investigating how Chi flow affects us. A part of understanding energy within Feng Shui theory is the awareness of our tendency to label things good or bad. In many of the before and after illustrations throughout the book better alternatives are suggested to increase our observations. It had been my experience that polarities create little room for solutions. Becoming familiar with these terms is to be informed should you come across them in other Feng Shui publications.

SI CHI : This is the movement of energy in a balanced, harmonious way. Si chi should flow into a space, meander around and pool before moving on. It will move on and out either the way in came in or through an alternative source such as a door or window.

SHENG CHI : is the movement of Chi that gets temporarily interrupted.

This can be a path that abruptly ends or a piece of furniture out of place. It eventually finds its way around the obstruction to find its balance again. When a person meets with Sheng Chi repetitively, it weakens the immune system.

SHA CHI : is a term that is used to describe energy that moves too fast, is stagnant or is a result of geopathic stress. Sha Chi is the opposite of Si Chi in how it is experienced. Examples: Accelerating speed on a straight highway or experiencing stale air in a closed room. Sha Chi drains or over stimulates the immune system which can have debilitating health affects. Feng Shui strives to minimize the affects of Sha Chi and maximize the benefit of Shi Chi. The goal is to create balanced and harmonious environments for optimal health and well being.

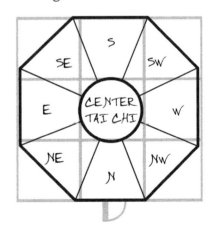

The Bagua 'octagon' is laid over a building to represent 9 spaces. Irregular shapes are evaluated individually. Each area is 1/9th of the whole.

FENG SHUI SCHOOLS and their relevance for the design professions

When applying Feng Shui theory in design and development professions it is necessary to determine if Form or Landscape takes precedence over Compass. The ideologies of both Schools of Feng Shui do overlap and can be relevant in any situation. Which is chosen will determine how the Bagua is placed and how much import is put on that placement.

For Architects, Designers and Decorators : When the goal is precision Traditional Compass School is the best place to start. Form School or 3 Door System can then be used as a backup to check what parallel energies may be present. For Architects this information is used to site buildings and balance exterior elements. The Bagua as a tool indicates directions, elements, their colors and how and where to balance them. Shapes of buildings, missing guas etc can have an impact on a design. Designers and decorators have more control over the interior spaces. They can bring balance and harmony to the elements by the use of color, furnishings and lighting. Architects can use the Bagua to macro site while decorators and designers microsite rooms and interior spaces.

The Bagua offers a new dimension to these professions.

For DEVELOPERS : Developers often have detailed lists of things to consider including access, water, power, positioning and shape of land. Feng Shui knowledge and application is valuable when considering project sites. Landscape Feng Shui is the optimal tool for evaluating land. Geophysical and environmental assessment can indicate geopathic stress, human memory imprints, cultural and historic activities of previous occupants. Geomancy, a key factor, is often overlooked when evaluating land developments and locating suitable entry points. Using the Bagua and geomantic knowledge expands a developer's vision.

For BUILDERS : Builders work either with architects/designers or directly with owners/clients. Builders who work directly with clients can influence the design process.

Using Landscape Feng Shui to check forms in the environment is an appropriate first step for builders. Knowing the importance of entrances and their placement can be key for the success of a project. A builder should check both the shape of the land and the shape of a building. The Bagua is then referenced to determine if missing

areas occur. Odd land shapes and irregular building placement can create disharmony. When a builder can align one wall of a structure to be parallel to one property line the building is considered grounded. Grounding is a metaphor for builders as it is they who create the foundation.

Fortunate Blessings # 4 SE	Vision # 9 SOUTH	Relationship # 2 SW
Ancestors # 3 EAST	Tai Chi Spirit # 5 CENTER	Creativity & Children # 7 WEST
Knowledge # 8 NE	Career # 1 NORTH	Helpful People & Travel # 6 NW

The Bagua energies described above are show here with the 3 Door System. With Compass School the direction/energy is applied appropriately, no matter where the door is located.

Grounding a Building:
Odd Shapes on Standard Lots

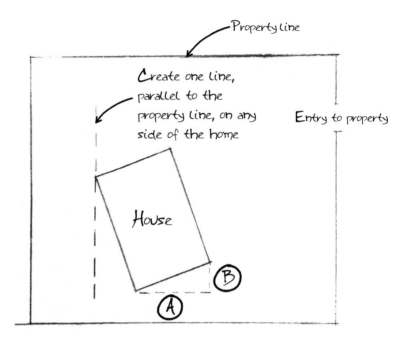

Ⓐ One side of the home should be parallel with the property line or boundary. If a dwelling is not aligned and located as seen here then the structure is not grounded on the land. Only one side of the structure needs to align with a property boundary.

Ⓑ There are many creative ways to make the parallel line. A simple row of rocks can achieve this. More aesthetic options include creating a garden area or constructing a deck. Creating a line or filling in the space will anchor the dwelling, creating grounding and balance.

CHI: The Esoteric to the Practical

In North America we are familiar with the elements Air, Fire, Water and Earth. Many First Nations and ancient cultures refer to these basic earth borne elements. Architects and developers site projects based on land orientation and compass directions. Where are the prevailing winds? Where is the sun's path through the sky? How does the land slope? Where is the view? Where should septic fields and access routes be located? One can have a basic understanding of elemental influences without the benefit of the Five Transformation Theory or knowing the relationship between geography and geomancy.

When orienting a building or ourselves within a building, we may not be compass-aware but we know the path of the sun. For those of us who live in the extreme northern or southern hemispheres, the sun's path is crucial to our wellbeing as we pass through the seasons. This Fire element represented by the sun is basic to survival. It is key in orienting, seeking and building shelter. All other elements fall in line: Earth as the foundation, Water an absolute necessity and Air (Wood/ Metal) forming a whole in the transformational process. Good Feng Shui and good design are synonymous. In the Western world we tend to experience the elements in a more linear and static way, often compartmentalizing their

effects on us. The Oriental viewpoint is more all encompassing as it views the elements in every aspect of life and overall health. This allows a more holistic approach when applying these concepts to design. The terms Energy, Chi, Prana or Qi refer to overall life force. In primitive and animistic cultures it is measured by what is 'becoming' in each moment, ever and always changing. This viewpoint reflects a dynamic interaction within the environment. Energy can be difficult to quantify and qualify. Perhaps it's not the good and bad that we have to decide upon, but our subjective experience of what is felt at any given time and place. This invites us to embrace a broader perspective; enriching the possibilities for new design and vision. When we apply the concepts of energy, flow and continuous change to design practices there is a fundamental shift. Embracing the notion of chi as continually changing is a Zen ideology. It allows us to drop into the moment and experience design as a more co-creative practice. In Asian cultures the Five Elemental Theory is a life long study as it embodies dynamic change. It explains the essence of Chi flow, which is a moment to moment experience. Labeling it good or bad creates polarization and judgement. These Eastern theories involve us in the experience by way of deep observation

and innovative response. All creative processes benefit and deepen when we overcome our static nature as the basis for dynamic movement. Applying these ideas to modern professions is challenging, yet it can be simple. Consider how we may perceive the energy of a church as opposed to a casino. When we simplify our observations by using Yin Chi and Yang Chi for comparison, we take away preconceived ideas and bypass evaluating what the spaces represent. Yin is associated with dark, sour, below, deep, mysterious and feminine principles. Yang's quality is opposite: bright, sweet, above, bold, obvious and masculine. When evaluating spaces from this perspective we discover what is needed to create balance. Understanding space by understanding its Yin or Yang quality can show us where polarities are created. The play of the five elements is a continual and fine balance of Yin and Yang, esoteric and complex perhaps, yet basic. The essence of Chi becomes the source of these opposites. Their expression is through the movement of the five elements or these five errant children who are always playing and interacting. At times the play is light and sometimes it's dark. These concepts are at the core of Feng Shui theory and allows our subjective experience to become more objective in its practice.

Gallery

Combinations of Elements

WOOD: Bamboo as a feature column, material in roof detail, support beam and greenery. FIRE is the roof shape.

34) METAL is represented in the spiral and WOOD in the height, pole and color.

EARTH walls of clay & stone floor.

35) The Petronas towers are METAL, (color) WOOD, (height) and FIRE (lighting).

36) WOOD and FIRE shape going towards a pointed triangulation getting increasingly small and the red color under the roof.

WOOD material of structure and its graduated height; rising up like a tree to the heavens.

37) METAL wash basin, Wood materials in a WATER area with the FIRE of the visionary (designer) and the colors of EARTH (browns and beiges).

FIRE dominates in the color red which creates a reverse triangle; FIRE'S symbol.

This photo evokes the elementals; the very core of Wind/ Water or Feng Shui.

Predominantly green of WOOD and the undulation of the rice fields represents WATER.

ALL ELEMENTS

38)

FIRE: *Peaked roofs*

EARTH: *Colors of roofs and sky*

METAL: *The arches formed in the reflection and curves of structure's edges*

WATER: *Water of the rice paddy and color blue*

WOOD: *Colors green, blue green, bamboo structures, trees*

Feng Shui Design expands the 'form follows function' concept to include chi flow as an added dimension.

The terms, concepts and theories from Sections One and Two expands
awareness of the energy that goes beyond aesthetics.

Developers envision it, Architects conceptualize it, Builders create it, Designers articulate it
and Decorators embellish it.

Whether applied to work or in everyday life there is an elemental role for everyone.

FENG SHUI APPLICATION: SPACE BY SPACE

ENTRANCES

Every space demands attention to the function it serves. Entrances to a city, landscape, property or home create an initial impact and a feeling. As such they are a crucial feature in design. The entrance is the start of our journey though land or a space. As a symbolic first impression it imparts vital information. Entrances are where personality is expressed.

Defining and creating good entrances to homes and businesses is the goal of Feng Shui design. Even though these main entrances may not be considered the Cosmic Mouth of Chi, or even the Energetic Front Door, they are still important. In Feng Shui Design a main entrance is where guests are received. Friends, clients and visitors alike relax when they have arrived at the right location and entry. Visible address identification, good lighting and signage contribute to a sense of security and arrival. All aspects of entry are felt as well as seen.

A pathway leading to an arbor creates a mystical sense of going beyond the ordinary.

An entry in Santa Fe, N.M. creates privacy and protection but offers beauty and welcome.

There is a distinction between entrances to homes and businesses. Entrances to homes should evoke a sense of arrival and relaxation. This is considered Yin Chi.

Entrances are powerful and symbolic in Feng Shui Design.

The purple gate is the security entry to two separate residences ~ Positive Feng Shui or not? If the careers of the owners are similar or if the two homes belong to members of the same family it could be very auspicious.

Photos of a this shared entry draws the eye to artwork, tiles, adobe inlay and a purple gate. Upon a closer look it reveals two separate residences.

Entrances To Properties

Entrances to properties are as important as main door entries. Finding a driveway is not often easy. Rural properties may have more than one entrance. Having reflective surfaces on signage, fire numbers and addresses are necessary in rural or obscure locations. Using landmarks, lighting and sculptures at the driveway entrance are also useful indicators. When a home or business is not visible from the entry or if a driveway is particularly long then visual indicators are important. Reflectors, placed at various increments assure a visitor arrival to a designated parking area. Adequate road width and maintenance are also essential for creating an inviting, safe arrival. Homes and businesses in rural areas have similar requirements for proper entry. Designated parking areas should be well lit with a definitive visual connection to where to enter buildings. If the entry to be used differs from the architectural main entrance then it must be made clear. Using plants, statues and or lighting will guide newcomers to the preferred entrance. Both home and business entrances need attention to safety. Good lighting along with defined and safe walkways are necessary, especially in climates that experience adverse weather conditions. A home based business owner must pay special attention to these factors for insurance purposes.

This dramatic entry draws attention and creates ambiance and mystery.

Experiences with Entrances
Part One: Where is it ?

Early in my Feng Shui Career I attended a workshop in California where I asked about entrances. The Feng Shui expert reminded me of the connection to career clarity. She also advised me to invite someone who had never been to my house, to visit and give me their impressions. Our home had a great view, in a private cozy setting in a small mountain town.

The first impression upon my friends visit was his confusion about how to get into the house. Although I was shocked, I understood. The realtor had led us as new purchasers into the home. This friend was invited to an address and had to find his way. When he did find the door his experience of the house overall was that of delight. Renovated prior to our purchase, the outside looked lovely but there was no real defined sense of entry other than a worn path to one door and a small basement entry under a deck. His visit opened my eyes and had me ask 'had my intuition been telling me there was a problem?'

The house was situated at the end of a steep street. There was a turnaround with no other homes at the top. The driveway came off the turnaround at a steep angle yet was easy to see. The house number was clear and the home simple to find. The only door visible was small and was under a deck that led to the basement. Although a worn path led around to what I considered the main entry, there was no indication of which entry to use. A grassy path led up one level and rounded a corner to a South facing kitchen/summer entry. Without a porch, using it during the snow months was limited. The small basement entry on the North side, sheltered by an overhead deck worked best in winter. This entrance provided room for outdoor gear, storage and acted as a buffer to the cold air. I never gave any thought as to how others would find it. Fresh eyes were able to point out the obvious. My first priority was to embellish the path. It was re-defined by lining it with river rock, filling it with gravel and placing plants, flowers and lights in strategic locations. After these changes had been made there was no doubt about where to go. The new path created a sense of mystery and invitation. It drew guests towards it and the small door under the deck went unnoticed.

This lesson became an important teaching tool over the years. I would advise students, when they had been away for several days or on holidays, to look at their entrances and interiors with new eyes. Writing one's first impression allows one to see. When accustomed to living in a home or apartment over time it is easy to ignore the broken doorbell, askew path tiles, or things that have worn out. All these small seemingly insignificant things start to drain energy and create confusion. When entrances are given a face lift it elevates the quality of Chi, making it welcoming.

The most important benefit took time to realize, but there was a shift in my Career. I made a definitive move to become a Feng Shui practitioner. I could now apply my expertise as a designer to practice this expanded art of placement. The confusion between the two doors, had me torn between whether to continue to travel and import or start my own business in design. When the entrance became clear, so did my career choice. In 1997 I started my own business as a Feng Shui Design Consultant. I've never looked back.

Optimal Entrances

The optimal entry is one that provides a complete 180 degree view looking out from the main door. In northern climates it is common to protect entrances with overhangs and covered roofs while maintaining a view.

House styles that feature covered wrap around porches give protection without obstructions. Recessed entranceways do not provide the expansive 180 degree view desirable for a good Feng Shui entry. Indented entranceways can create blockages on the right, left or on both sides of an entrance. Standing while looking out of a door is how to apply the Landscape Feng Shui model. It is used to determine the male/female balance. Dragon energy on the left relates to adult males. Tiger energy on the right relates to adult females. Detecting imbalance in adult relationships can be pinpointed at a main entry, especially one that is recessed. When the Tiger is blocked the male is dominant. When the Dragon is blocked the female energy is dominant. The object of the 180 degree view is to support male/female harmony. In situations where women live without men or vice versa this is less important. The large wall on the left or Dragon side and a smaller wall to the right or Tiger side, show that both are blocked. This affects both the males and females living there. A door with a full 180 degree view provides the conditions for a healthy viable relationship and powerful Chi to enter a space.

Garage competes with a recessed entrance, which in Landscape Feng Shui, blocks the Tiger.

A curved path to a slightly indented entry is the better option for good Landscape Feng Shui.

A recessed entrance blocks the dragon side of this home.

Although the main feature of the house is a garage, the entrance on the upper floor is 180 degrees and is sheltered.

The line of trees blocks the Ming Tang of the front entrance of this home, creating obstacles.

Entrances and Career

Occupants, visitors, and clients are impacted by what they encounter at an entrance. Feng Shui teaches the importance of creating awareness and intention. The entry opens to an experience or a Journey. The 3 Door System allocates the front door as North, NW or NE. When the door is central it is directly aligned with North, the # 1 and the Journey on the Bagua compass. In Feng Shui this corresponds to the Journey through life, symbolized by Career. This can be interpreted in broad terms but essentially what we do in life that sustains us.

Business Entrances

Businesses are Yang in nature. They require a more activated Chi flow to attract people. The nature of the business and the location are factors when considering its entrance. Appropriate signage and good lighting play a crucial role in the entry. In Feng Shui, corner locations attract the most traffic for retail sales. A corner allows for an angled entrance that draws in energy from multiple directions. The best Feng Shui and activated Chi occurs when a business faces south or is on the sunny side of the street. The power of the sun's energy draws more traffic in general. Should an establishment be on the shade side of the street lighting can make a difference when attracting customers. Lighting is a physical aspect of the Fire element; it is noticed above other elements. The color red, the angular shapes or corner entrances evoke Fire, vision and being seen. Retail businesses should invite clients to engage. The symbology at an entrance should reflect prosperity, ease and a level of sophistication that suits what is offered beyond the door. When entrances for businesses are dingy, have poor, dysfunctional lighting or doors that stick, squeak or are not visually attractive they send unwelcoming messages to clients. Consider the first impression created at the entry to your business, make an assessment and have clients give feedback.

Home Business Entrances and Locations

When a business is located in a home, the active Yang energy and restful Yin must be balanced. More and more people work from their homes but the distractions of domestic life can be a challenge. Homes are for rest and businesses are for activity. Separating these activities by the entrance location can be key in its success. Placing a home based business in an adjacent building serves several purposes. First, this allows for a separation of the active Yang energy needed to sustain work and the restful Yin quality needed for the home space. If this is not possible, having a business office close to a front door allows the chi arriving to be channeled into the work space. Visitors to the business will not have to enter personal space and the business will benefit from the more active yang chi that arrives at the entry. Businesses require concentration, focus and creativity. Should a home business be located within the home away from an entry, Yang Chi is still required. Color and lighting can activate an office and the passage way to it. Regardless, the many things that affect a public business affect home businesses. Creative use of signage for a home business can direct the chi towards the work area and away from the private space. Sound separation can be a factor, especially if there are children in the home during business hours. External factors such as well lit addresses, rural fire numbers, clear signage and clean, safe, attractive paths and driveways become crucial in good Feng Shui design. Creative solutions to these issues will attract and assure repeat business. Even when your home based business is internet based, having distinct and clear separation from the home increases productivity.

Entrances and Chi flow in Large Buildings

Chi flowing into larger buildings is strongest at the main entry. The effects differ between office, retail and living spaces. Offices close to the entrance allows energy to infuse the work space and is auspicious for retail businesses. Businesses at the furthest location from an entry may not prosper as energy is minimized. If businesses receive external energy via a good view, energy source is external and they may do better than businesses that do not.

Home spaces located in apartments should be restful, while escaping external influences. An apartment near a front entrance may not be as quiet as one further away. Apartments mid building are best. Like an office or retail space, apartments with a view or Ming Tang allows cosmic chi from the atmosphere to balance energy.

Chi Flow Through Apartment and Office Buildings

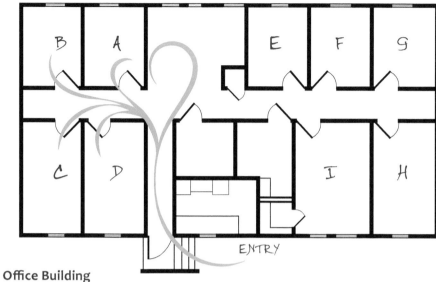

Office Building

The chi flows to units A and D first then to units C and D. These will be the most energized office units in the building.

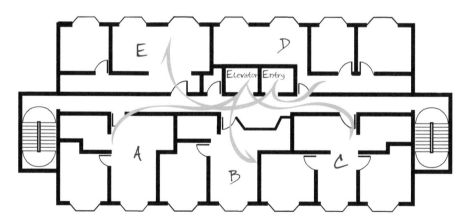

Apartment Building : Upper floor

Units on an upper floor closest to the elevator, get the most energy. Good but less dynamic chi flow is optimal for living spaces. Units B, D and E get stronger chi than Units A and C. As the floors go up, apartments buildings are energized by external atmospheric chi.

FOR HOME BUSINESS

- Will the yin quality of the restful home be affected by a home office?
- What percentage of clients come to your home business if you are primarily on line?
- Does the entry to your office evoke professionalism by being clear of clutter?
- Is your home office entrance well lit and clear?
- Is the home office near the entry of the home or buried deep in a back bedroom?
- Does your home office have a good Ming Tang, or symbology such as photos of landscapes that inspire to allow you to expand into the vision for the business?
- Is there enough active or Yang energy to keep your home business energized?
- Will the business impact others negatively such as family or neighbours with service trucks, noise etc.?
- Is the type of business appropriate to have in a home location?
- Is it awkward to take clients through personal space to your home office?
- Is your home business easily found by clients?

FOR COMMERCIAL PUBLIC BUSINESSES

- Is your business in a well trafficked area?
- Does the business have good signage and lighting?
- Is the business easy to find?
- Does your business have sufficient active Yang energy to inspire its development and attract potential clients?
- Does the entry attract passers by who could be clients?
- Is the business entry free from clutter?
- Is the business entrance attractive to customers ?

An optimal business entry: An angular entry is both a feature and attracts energy from two directions at once.

- Are there water features near the front door or in the business?
- Are these water features positioned to attract abundance? A pool or circular flow in a wood gua is best.
- Are water features positioned to drain the abundance? Water flow that points out the door instead of inward.
- Are water features in an area that would not work well with the element water? Earth guas control water and wealth.

East VS West Business Entrances

Bold and modern makes indentification of this bookstore easy.

The Arc, a metaphysical bookstore in New Mexico has an appealing sign and an intriguing entrance. The direct path to the door is softened by adobe gateway and cascading plant. These features give a sense of passing into another dimension, like the Asian moon gate below.

A standard concrete building in Narita, Japan is transformed and made inviting to customers by the addition of colour, lighting, wood, earth and plants. It draws us in although not particularly slick or fancy.

This Asian 'moon gate' invites the visitor to cross over into a lush environment and out of the concrete city. A moongate's design is to purposely beckon one to enter; passing from the normal to the mystical.

A welcoming entry with obvious curved path.

A Modern home with trees that will block out the Ming Tang in future.

A curved path to entry hidden by bushes.

A simple entry that provides shelter, but lack of a landing at the door creates an unstable entry in spite of railing. This entrance creates a feeling of protection and welcome.

This South West style is also without a landing outside. The adobe wall, flowers and wider steps create stability and a pleasant feel to this entrance.

Experiences with Entrances
Part Two: Career and Entry

After I had been a practitioner for over 7 years I had another revelation about entrances. I had just returned from my first tutelage under Feng Shui Grandmaster Dr. Jes Lim. Finding him as a teacher at that time was pivotal. In just a few days I learned new things about Landscape Feng Shui, the Lopan and entrance energy. I was about to reevaluate entry and career!

He taught the concept of Ming Tang, which in my home was on the NW, opposite to my main door at the SE and what I considered the Cosmic Mouth of Chi although it faced a mountain. The door to the deck had a great lake view and better Ming Tang. It was time to reevaluate the front door yet again. To activate the deck entry and Ming Tang as the actual front entrance, stairs to it were required.

I excitedly chatted about what I was learning with my husband via phone as I was in San Francisco studying. This new information was a catalyst for change. I was gone for one week and when I returned the deck was gone. It was old and needed replacement and the only way to access it was via the interior of the house. The plan now was to create a stairway to the deck from the driveway. This would not only invite the Chi to enter on the same side as the Ming Tang but it would allow Chi to flow up the stairs to the newly activated front sliding glass door. Although I had created a definitive entrance years before, the small door to the basement was still visible. With a new deck complete this small winter entry door was no longer visible.

I recalled how my Career became solidified 7 years before by activating my SE entrance. I was curious about what would happen with a totally new NW entrance. As a West Life person, NW was a better direction for me. SW was my spouse's direction as an East Life person. In the next few months everything shifted. My Career became activated in a way I had not imagined.

Having just returned from my study with Master Lim, I knew he had activated me and my passion for the work in a new way. This was his first and perhaps only visit to North America. I wanted to continue to study with him but my funds were limited. Within 2 weeks I found the resources to continue studying with Dr Lim. What I thought would be a one time only meeting with a master, became my path.

My Feng Shui design career shifted into high gear over the ensuing years as I continued to study with Dr Lim. I received part one of my diploma in Toronto. I went on to finish my Feng Shui diploma in Spain the following spring. I studied Geomancy and Feng Shui for Business the next summer in Mexico city. A few years later I travelled to Austria to study Zen/Tao Garden Design with my European colleagues. Dr. Lim's work led me to my dowsing master Eric Dowsett. To this day, I continue to be inspired by the work of Grand Master Jes Lim and I am a member of his organization: Qi Mag International.

CONFUSION VS BLOCKAGES AT ENTRANCE WAYS

There is a distinct difference between confusion and a blockage at an entry.

Confusion is when a visitor does not know how to find the entrance. Entrances that are obscured with trees or other natural overgrowth, not properly marked or well lit, can be easily missed. Confusion at an entry is unsettling and unwelcoming for visitors. Metaphorically in Feng Shui, this can have a direct link to being confused about one's livelihood or career.

Blockages can be physical or energetic. There are several ways to determine blockages at an entrance and places to look out for them.

Visible Clues

Visible clues that can indicate both electromagnetic and geophysical interference.

- Power poles, lines and transformers.
- Electricity panels near an entry.
- Visual clues indicating geophysical blockages.
- Land depressions.
- Grass discoloration or lack of growth.
- Trees that have unnatural bends; these can indicate geophysical anomalies such as water and fault lines or a combination of several underground stress factors.

Tree placement directly in front of the main entrance blocks chi from inside and out. Chi is directed at garage doors, creating confusion and adding to the blockage.

First : Blockages can occur at the entrance to a piece of land or property or en route to a building entrance. Examples of physical blockages are plant overgrowth or entrances that are too narrow. When we come across areas that restrict Chi flow it can be felt physically and emotionally. Underground radiation emanating from natural sources such as water lines, fault lines, and mineral deposits can affect Chi flow at entrances. Metaphysical and electromagnetic disturbances can also block energy at an entry. People with heightened sensitivities may feel these more than others. Trained geomancers will use dowsing tools to check the energy at an entrance for these phenomena.

Electromagnetic blockages at doorways can result in headaches, temporary dizziness or disorientation. This may minimize for occupants over time as they get used to the electromagnetic radiation. The harm is not eliminated as it will stress the immune system.

Second : Blockages that can be seen or felt while arriving at a building or a home. These can also occur right at a doorway or an entrance. Physical blockages are obvious when approaching a destination or an entry.

Chi flow is affected by what we see and feel. Watch out for:

- overflowing garbage and odors
- prominent and or unsightly recycle bins
- pathways that are too narrow or are in disrepair
- items left in a pathway or doorway (toys, garden tools, utility items, sport gear)
- poor lighting
- inadequate signage

Natural occurring geomantic energies can block or divert Chi from entering a property or building. Dowsers will use tools when checking for unseen phenomena. The procedure is to walk past the door or entrance while concentrating on following the chi. The path of chi should flow naturally into the entrance. When the dowsing tool pulls away from an entrance it is a strong indication that the chi is blocked. Such blockages are caused by Geophysical, Metaphysical or Electromagnetic interference.

A common metaphysical occurrence is the repetitive use of an entrance by an occupant. Humans, habitual by nature create energetic pathways known as human memory imprints, also referred to as ley lines. When a personal ley line is interrupted it creates a disturbance in the habitual pattern. When a blockage is physical the object can be removed; such as a toy in a driveway or garbage receptacles left on the curb.

Third : Blockages as viewed from the inside of a main entrance looking out tend to be more physical in nature. Chi must flow as easily out of a space as in. When looking out from a main entrance Ming Tang comes into play. Entrances that face a wall, building, fence or prominent natural features like trees and hedges will limit vision.

The Feng Shui metaphor for visual blockages outside an entrance is related to what impedes moving forward in life. The idea of Ming Tang is to have a clear vision.

Symbolically we need to be able to see where we are going. Obstacles such as trees and bushes may be easily removed or pruned. Large buildings or walls close to a main entrance are not easily moved. Finding an alternative entrance is then necessary to open up the possibilities for the occupants. The quality of Chi that flows onto land and into buildings can affect the level of health and energy of occupants and users. Entrances into multi use buildings impact activities and visitors arriving there. Small issues often get over looked. Fixing broken screens, door latches, squeaky doors, replacing broken door bells, light fixtures and bulbs are examples of quick and easy remedies. Minor renovations and painting are sometimes required to shift energy at an entry. More involved solutions can be time consuming and costly yet necessary when energy flow is compromised.

Good design and development creates good if not great entrances! Healthy buildings depend on many factors overall. A well designed entrance does not insure an energized healthy building, but it is a good start.

Chi Flow from the Road into a Property

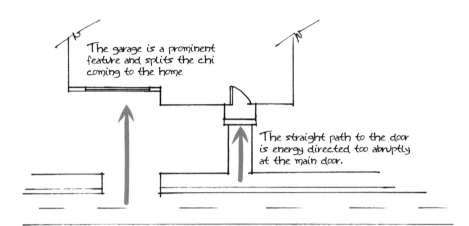

The garage is a prominent feature and splits the chi coming to the home

The straight path to the door is energy directed too abruptly at the main door.

Unfavourable Feng Shui

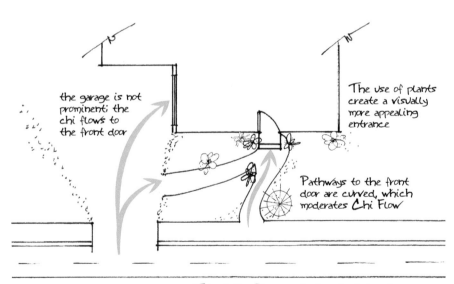

the garage is not prominent; the chi flows to the front door

The use of plants create a visually more appealing entrance

Pathways to the front door are curved, which moderates Chi Flow

Tail of the Dragon principle is obvious here

Favourable Feng Shui

How Entrances Impact Design and Development

Creating energized entrances can have long lasting effects. Whether you are a developer starting with a fresh piece of land or a decorator trying to remedy a client's disaster, there are many ways to create solutions at challenged entrances. Often what we find at the entrance to a property geophysically, cannot be changed. If Chi cannot be directed in a positive way to sites or buildings, they may not be optimal to develop. The creativity of the architect, builder or designer can influence the energy at entrances. The goal is to maximize the client's experience while improving the success of the project. Promoting optimal health and well being for residents, clients and potential buyers is a responsibility that all design and development professions share.

For Developers: The scale of the project, logistics, budget and location, are some of the main factors for developing land. For developers, the entrance to the land is as important as the buildings. Simple things can shift energy such as the orientation of a front door and developing potential views. Land carries much information that can be accessed by dowsing. Discerning potential from challenges is imperative for developers. It can be as simple as a slight movement in siting a building which will enhance optimal energy, especially at the entrance.

For Builders: What applies to developers is also true for builders. Easy access to protected building entrances that are free of confusion and blockages is crucial. Views and orientation of Ming Tang is another check point. Builders can improve challenging entrances by creating a microcosm of natural beauty. The addition and use of lighting, sculptures, plants and water features can take the focus off unfavourable exterior influences. A builder can create activating and positive Chi flow by improving an entry's design.

For Architects: Architects have a natural capacity to create great entries. The work starts with gathering information which translates into a great plan. Shifting the focus from garage entrances to a front door activates the energy when the door is used. Eliminating structural blockages and optimizing Ming Tang will also open up possibilities for occupants. Correcting challenges on a floor plan saves money and increases the prosperity of all involved. Satisfied clients lead to success and referrals.

39) Urban coffee shop entrance reveals a corner door and colors that are inviting.

For Designers: Designers can rectify poor entrances in a myriad of ways. Changing the direction a door faces, by checking the East Life/West life information of clients, is one option. Shifting the energy of an entrance draws upon creativity, experience and knowledge. Feng Shui Design refers to elemental knowledge to enhance the energy at an entrance while personalizing it for the client. A good entry sets the stage for creative interior design and optimal chi flow.

For Decorators: Using color, form and shape when enhancing an entrance leaves a lasting impact. A decorator can use a good design as a backdrop for creating harmony. Balancing directions and elements will shift energy at an entrance. A decorator's job is to personalize the entry for clients while guiding them in the process.

Remedial Entry Design from an Interior Perspective

40) Before

40) After

Yang energy is required for this well marked home business. Staggering planters on each side of entrance will soften any poison arrow effect of a direct driveway.

Garages and Entrance Ways

In North America many home designs feature the garage as a focal point. As practical as this is, it minimizes the power of a main entry. There are many great designs that incorporate functional garages as a secondary feature. Locating them to the side or having them recessed, keeps the focus on the main entry. Older areas of cities that are redeveloped have better entrances due to back alley access. Alleys are a practical solution for parking, garbage, recycling and storage of outdoor utility items. The front door becomes a focal point in this type of planning. When the prominent entry is through a garage, how is the front door activated? The only way to maintain the front door as the main entrance is to use it daily. If the Ming Tang or Energetic Front Door is not at the main entrance this is a lesser issue. Feng Shui Design seeks to be creative in the entrance vs garage debate while honouring a function that has become a requirement in many countries.

The garage is visible yet not the feature of this modern design.

East Life vs West Life: Directions and Entrances

If occupants live in a home that faces West and they are all born with East Life influences, the home is not optimal for them. In such a case Landscape can take precedence if it is balanced according to the Landscape Feng Shui animals and elements. Regardless, determine where Cosmic Mouth of Chi enters the house in a direction compatible with the clients. This is where the energy arrives to the home from the environment through a window or door. Invite the energy in to the home from the directions that resonate with the occupants. Focus on Western directions for West Life and Eastern directions for East Life clients. Inviting the energy in is the activating principle and can be done by spending time at that location. Problematic cases could require renovations or a possible relocation.

Using the Elemental Birth Chart allows us to look at the overall elements and optimal client directions. Birth elements for occupants show us how well they fit with a home or office space.

Landscape Feng Shui and the Cosmic mouth of Chi can then either support an activation or not. Activating the Cosmic Mouth of Chi is possible, whether it is an entrance, a window or an opening to a deck. When a view or Ming Tang aligns with client directions, energy is amplified. Note that it is a problem only if all occupants do not match the home direction.

A Typical Catalogue or Mail Order House Plan

Five major issues: Typical catalogue homes

- The right side of the main entrance is blocked which blocks the Tiger energy. This may affect females in the home.

- The left side of the entry blocks the Dragon energy and can affect the males in the home. It is a smaller block than the Tiger side so females will be compromised more in this design.

- The garage is a more dominant feature than the entrance.

- The energy arriving at the main door will escape directly through to the other side when the door is opened.

- The back entrance has a stairwell directly off to the side which if not separated by a door, is A) extremely dangerous, B) pulls the chi down into the lover level.

Note: Its optimal in Feng Shui Design to have a 180 degree view from the front door so as to see in all directions and have a clear view to Ming Tang. Keeping this in mind note this in this example.

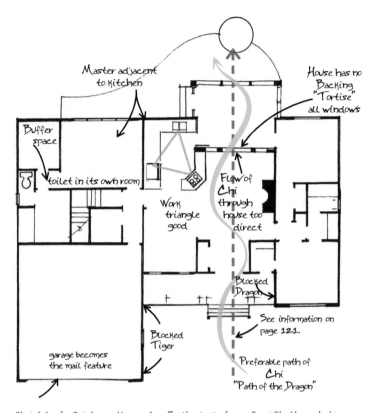

Sketch is of a Catalogue House. An effective test of your Feng Shui knowledge.

FENG SHUI DON'TS

- At the entry two features stand out to a trained eye. The first is the garage door. In many North American homes this is a major exterior feature and draws unnecessary attention. In Feng Shui the chi and attention should be primarily directed to the front door.

- Next is how the garage protrudes from the face of the home, creating a recessed entry. This design feature protects the door from the elements. In Feng Shui we use creative solutions to suit climatic needs and minimize compromising Chi flow at the entry. To apply Landscape Feng Shui stand at the front door looking out and take note of the animal positions to evaluate the symbology.

- Here the Dragon /male/yang and Tiger/female/yin energies are blocked on both sides. Although the Dragon is less so, over time this may create problems in the outer world for both the males and females who occupy the home. In this example, the Tiger is more disadvantaged so females in the home can be challenged with work and health. A remedy is to put a reflective surface, such as a mirror, on either side of the doorway. The goal is to be able to see what is happening on the street. Surfaces that work on exteriors as mirrors are burnished copper, aluminum and flat metal sculptures.

- From the entry the Chi moves directly from the foyer through the home to the outside patio. There is no allowance for Chi to pool or gather in the space. When Chi moves rapidly and escapes rapidly, the residents will not benefit. A more serpentine flow through the space can be created by using furnishings, artwork, mirrors and lighting. The Tail of the Dragon meanders and allows residents to slow down and feel rested in the space.

- Note the location of the study/bedroom. Being close to the front door, it works well as a guest room. Guests will not stay longer than you wish them to. It can serve as a home business office as clients can access the space without going into the home. Using it as a child's bedroom is not favourable unless it is an older child who is ready to leave home. Young children should be closer to their parents and not have bedrooms near entrances.

- The garage location creates a missing area from the overall interior layout. The protrusion of the garage from the floor plan and the fact that it is external, are both issues. Bagua placement determines which area is affected.

- The kitchen and master bedroom share a wall in this design. Sound attenuation is crucial in a home yet here the Yang energy of a kitchen space is in direct conflict with the Yin of a bedroom which should be restive and quiet. Materials used for wall construction and wall thickness will determine how much of an issue it is. Location of plumbing /wet wall is a key factor here.

FENG SHUI DOS

- The work triangle is well laid out in the kitchen. The cook is able to see guests and family members while working. There is ample counter space and room for more than one person to prep food.

- The master bedroom en suite has the toilet in its own room. The Yin energy of the toilet is distanced from the sleeping space. Although it could be further separated, being enclosed in its own space is good. The small hallway into the washroom and dressing room creates a good buffer.

- The extra screened in porch creates a small addition that amplifies this area of the home. Note that too large an extension or addition onto a home can create challenges. The energy of that particular Gua may become over energized. For example: The West Gua is the area of relaxation and pleasure /creativity and children. A large extension could promote overspending spending on leisure activities. A missing Gua here could limit occupants from having leisure time, children or creative outlets in their lives.

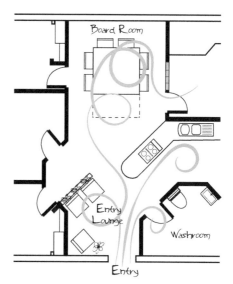

Chi in a well designed facility should meander through the space. Slowing down and arriving in various locations.

Spaces Above Garages

Although common, designing living spaces over garages in not favourable in Feng Shui design. There are a few things to consider. Many garages have overhead motors that operate the doors. These are noisy and have electromagnetic emissions which can be disturbing for those living above them. Vehicles emit fumes and unless there is a very strong protective barrier these emissions can reach living areas. Garages are often used for other functions such as workshops or storage areas. When these spaces become cluttered and dirty they can cause disturbances to those living above them.

Entering a Home

Getting past the front door into a home or building should be easy and inviting for everyone. There should be a discernible transition as one moves from the outer world into the sanctuary of a home. Entry areas should be uncluttered and appealing. Having closets nearby keep the area tidy, providing storage for clothing and other household objects. The Feng Shui as one enters is important. Bagua placement indicates the specific universal energy and element at the entry whether one chooses the Traditional Compass or the 3 Door Method. How Chi flows and pools inside an entry, home or business is determined by the design.

HALLWAYS AND STAIRWAYS

Hallways and stairways inside an entry are challenging features when there is not a defined foyer or reception area. Hallways and stairways can alter the chi flow depending on their location, placement or function. In a home energy flow is amped up when a long hallway or a stairway is immediately inside. In a business, hallways and stairways direct chi flow to various areas. When there is no reception area, a stairway and hallway locations become vital to how Chi is directed. When either are located at an entrance their visual impact is the first to inform us. Designing such a building must be well considered.

CHI FLOW INTO HOMES

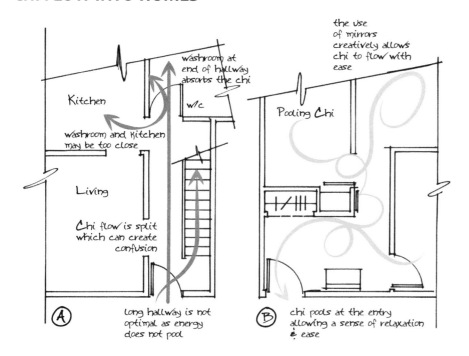

These illustrations show how chi / energy floes into different spaces.

Option A shows the chi being accelerated as long hallways direct chi in a straight line not allowing it to pool. Energy moves quickly away from the door not allowing a sense of arrival. The stairway creates another issue as the chi is split. This creates a deficiency of positive chi on the main floor. Note the washroom location. When directly across or adjacent to an entry, chi is drained. Whatever chi not sent to the upper floor is directed towards the washroom. Toilets and washrooms near or in a direct view line of an entry is unfavourable. Its Yin nature depletes chi due to odour and bacteria.

Option B is a preferable entrance. The chi at the entry pools and then moves on. The best of designs allow a feeling of relaxation at the entrance to a home. Care must be taken when using mirrors at a front entry. Locating one directly across from a front door can send the chi right back out. When placed beside an entry door or in a hallway, it can direct chi optimally through a space.

Hallways

Hallways allow for flow and circulation within a space. In Feng Shui design the object is to create the tail of the dragon; a soft curvaceous stream through a home or workplace. Hallways should take us on a journey in an easy, punctual fashion. Avoiding long hallways at an entry way is preferred. The objective is for energy to slow you down. In house design hallways are best off set from the main door. This allows visitors and occupants to become oriented. Long hallways are at times inevitable. Energy tends to move too quickly creating a funnelling effect. This can be unsettling and tedious. Lighting, color, proper art and mirror placement can direct the chi flow in a more subdued manner that reduces anxiety.

Hallways

Hallway One ~ The issue

This example shows a classic split vision. It occurs when the eye tries to focus on two surfaces; one closer and one further. Initially this may go unnoticed but over time an imbalance can occur affecting the immune system or the eyes. Placing a plant or a screen to keep both eyes focused on the same plane of vision is effective. The second challenge in illustration A is a Poison Arrow. This occurs when a sharp corner points directly at someone entering a space. In many modern designs such corners are now softly rounded, mitigating this effect. Poison arrows are not only an issue at doorways but where any sharp corner points directly at human bodies for short or long periods. It is optimal to adjust them or your position if you frequent a space where they occur.

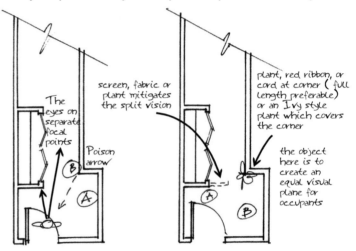

Hallway Two ~ The solution

One plane of vision creates a focal point for the eye. Fabric hanging from the ceiling or a small partition screen is a simple fix. Another efficient solution is to put a tall potted plant at that corner to create a different focal point. Eliminating a poison arrow can be as simple as hanging a red cord down the corner with the offending arrow. Do this only if it creates an attractive embellishment not an unfavourable distraction. The color red disperses the energy of the arrow. Plants are a good option for cures: Ivy or climbing plants work for eliminating the poison arrow but a larger plant would be needed for the split vision.

Comparing Home Entrances
Stairways at Entrances

These three examples show what happens when chi flowing into a space is spit and divided. When chi goes to an upper or lower floor at an entrance, the chi on the main floor is reduced. In the case of apartments in multileveled buildings, this can be an advantage if you are an occupant of an apartment on the second level. Other Illustrations point out various examples of stairways near entrances.

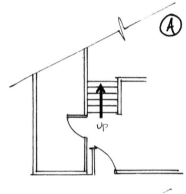

Sketch A
The energy flows directly up the stairs and has little time to pool on the first floor.

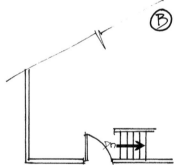

Sketch B
The energy of stairs adjacent to the door going to a lower level drains energy.

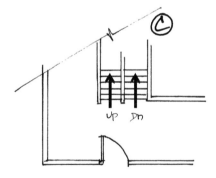

Sketch C
This sketch illustrates two things. First, stairwells to an upper and lower floor divides the energy close to the entry. Second, it illustrates a split level home which can create ups and downs in the occupants lives.

Stairways in an Entry

Stairways directly across from a doorway pulls the energy upward. It directs Chi to the upper floor and deprives it from entering the main floor. A stairway off to the side but close to an entry splits the chi into separate pathways. Stairs to a lower level adjacent to an entry are physically dangerous if there is no door. When energy is drawn down or up there is no place for it to pool. This can create unsettled feelings or subliminal confusion for those who enter. Occupants do adjust to the phenomena but over time it creates a drain on the immune system.

ESCAPING ENERGY

A classic faux pas in Feng Shui is to have the energy flow out of a home or space right after it arrives. The concept of pooling chi is what allows the body's immune system to arrive, relax and rejuvenate. Foyers and entry halls allow for this. Many modern homes are designed with larger windows and greater access to external views. Chi flows inward and outward through windows and doors. When a view is the primary feature upon entrance, it quickly diverts the focus from the interior to the exterior, accelerating the chi out of the building. A feature view should be slowly revealed otherwise energy has not time to settle into a space. Optimum designs allow chi to arrive in a gentle manner, with a great view being part of the discovery and enjoyment of a space. Creative manipulation of chi flow is possible when Feng Shui cures, such as plants, lighting, screens and special features are implemented.

41) Chi entering this building passes quickly through and exits the other side. The Feng Shui fix was to create a feature wall which diverted and pooled the chi, sending it around a corner to slowly meander through the space before leaving through the windows on the far side.

CHI FLOW DIRECTLY THRU A HOME

The main issue with this house design is the Escaping Chi. It flows directly from the main entrance through the house and out the back door like a gust of wind. Chi can also move like wind or Feng. Thinking of air flow can give us an idea of how chi/energy/prana moves through spaces. Optimal Chi pools and gathers. It allows a slow reveal of a home's features. The Pooling Chi areas in the sample are best in the living room and kitchen.

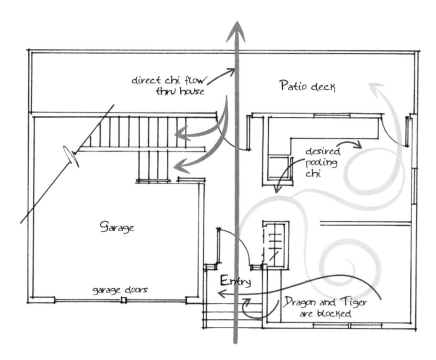

direct chi flow
thru house

Patio deck

desired
pooling
chi

Garage

garage doors

Entry

Dragon and Tiger
are blocked

When a door is too close to stairways, chi escapes towards them. Stairways at entries can divert chi away from the main floor. The exception is in apartment or office buildings where chi is directed to occupants via stairways.

THE HEART OF THE HOME

The center of a building is often referred to in Feng Shui as the Heart or Sacred Center. This is where we welcome a calm and clutter free environment. The three design features that we do not want to find in the center of a building are stairways, fireplaces or washrooms. Stairs are circulation areas and transfer energy from one floor to another. A washroom moves energy down via draining and flushing water. Fire places transfer heat up and out. The up and down motion of people, water or fire impedes the pooling of chi at the heart space. When the Chi is not able to pool in the center of a home it escapes both physically and symbolically. This area should be enjoyable and nurturing. The fire element is considered too dynamic an energy to be in a central location. Mirrors have been placed over fireplaces as a design feature for centuries. A mirror acts to reflect the energy back into the room. This not only acts as a Feng Shui cure but is a design standard. When employing a dowser to detect the heart of a home we may find the 'energy' of the heart has shifted to a gathering space such as a kitchen. Drawing a line from opposing corners on a floor plan to find where they intersect is a good indication of the center. Odd shaped buildings may require further investigation. See Section One, page 28.

Heart energy in a home is an esoteric concept. In Feng Shui we typically locate this at the center point of a room or a building. However, it is often found in places where families share time and space. On the Bagua the location is known as the Tai Chi or sacred center, where human and spiritual energy converge. When placing the Bagua, no matter what Feng Shui School is employed, the center remains the same. Although the Tai Chi will have its location, heart energy may shift to where frequent sharing and spiritual connections are made. In some cases the heart energy can be blocked. In older homes the heart energy can be found locked into a wall. Mental, physical and emotional disturbances from previous or current occupants can create this phenomena. When the heart energy of the home is blocked or disturbed, it can affect the persons who spend the most time there or play the most nurturing role. Emotional stress or physical disturbances such as heart conditions can result. Geomantic energy clearing can be effective in shifting this phenomena.

How to Expose a View

This Feng Shui house design shows a solution for when a view is a major feature in a home. Note that the Energetic Front door is not at the arrival entry but is the one that opens onto the front deck. This deck entry is an activated front door and facing the Cosmic Mouth of Chi and Ming Tang. As a new build, the street facing entrance will be the one where visitors arrive. The view across a valley is the main feature. A meandering path of chi goes from entry to feature wall, leading one to the kitchen, dining and living room prior to the view being revealed. The Tail of the Dragon is the basis for this Feng Shui design. Chi is allowed to pool while each area creates delight as it is discovered. The entire Feng Shui house design is featured in full in the Gallery for this section.

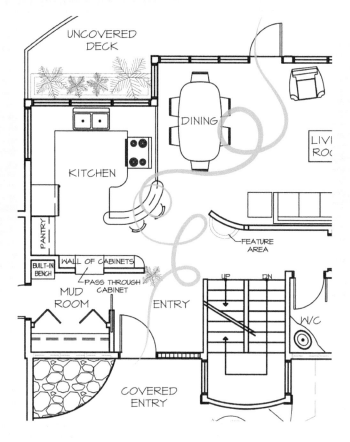

KITCHENS and GETTING ELEMENTAL

Kitchens nurture us physically making them the most frequented space in a house. The heart of a home often transfers to the kitchen as it is where family and friends gather, prepare and share food. In Feng Shui design we take special note of the elements Fire, Water and Metal in the kitchen. The element Fire is what cooks food as in a stove, oven or cooktop. The Water element has many functions in a kitchen. It is used to clean and prep food as well as making ice in most refrigerators. The Metal element is present in the fixtures appearing on stoves, refrigerators, cooktops and sinks. Creating nourishing meals provides us with health and well being. The alchemy of cooking using these elements symbolizes their importance. Their placement in Feng Shui design is of great significance.

The Fire element and the appliances that represent it become a focal point in a kitchen. Placement of appliances is vital in Feng Shui design. The danger associated with Fire begs that the cook be relaxed and in control. Having one's back to circulation within a kitchen prevents a cook from seeing what's going on behind them. When the cook cannot see who enters while prepping food it can be both unsettling and possibly dangerous. Locating a stove against a wall finds the cook's back turned away from the energy flow. Kitchen islands that include stove tops place the cook in the best position to engage with others in a relaxed manner.

Although **Water** is an important element in a kitchen, having one's back turned while at the sink is less dangerous than when cooking at a stove. Windows located in front of a sink, allows for natural light, relaxation and the ability to look out. This option is both good design and good Feng Shui. Kitchens are natural gathering areas where we celebrate life so people gravitate to them.

The stove top in an island is optimal Feng Shui as it allows the cook to be interactive with guests and family. The cook's back is not turned away.

Kitchen Locations

The optimal Feng Shui Kitchen placement in a home is East or South East. This is where the sun rises and it is also the location of the Wood element. Wood placed between Water in the North and Fire in the south creates harmony and flow. Where the sun comes up is the most Yang or active area in a home. E/ SE is bright in the morning. Whether the sun is visible or not its energy is felt on this side of a building. The quality of awakening evokes a more active energy infusing the food prepared. Play space near or in kitchens oriented in the E/SE can be advantageous. For children it serves as a place to be active and close to parents. Eastern facing rooms are energized, active and generate a creative flow through them. A dark north facing kitchen will have a more Yin quality. It is necessary to bring in the more active Yang principle in these locations for energized food preparation. North kitchens need special consideration in regards to lighting, ventilation and color to activate energy. North facing kitchens with limited light are generally colder which can lead to dampness and mould. When kitchens are placed in the north of buildings the energy is lower and time spent there is reduced. When this is the case it acts against the function of kitchen; that of being a gathering and nourishing space. Bright colors and warm lighting choices are a few remedies for such kitchens. Yin energy is quiet, internal, and isolated. It is associated with midnight and winter which lacks the stimulation necessary for kitchens. Many factors limit developers of apartments and condos as far as kitchen locations are concerned. Special attention given to the decor of North kitchens will pay off in the long run.

42)

The Work Triangle

Understanding a good kitchen work triangle is standard for designers, architects and developer/ builders. Functionality should never play second to aesthetics in a kitchen. The work triangle is created by the pathway between the refrigerator, sink and the cooktop/stove. It should allow for ease of movement in and around appliances and fixtures while giving ample counter top preparation space. Optimal work triangles are not excessively large which serves to reduce fatigue. Form Follows Function; this standard phrase in design is most important in the kitchen. As such, the work triangle is the starting point for good kitchen design. Making food prep enjoyable and efficient requires sufficient functional counter space. Triangles that are unnecessarily large can be exhausting for those working there. Layouts that are small or cramped are frustrating. A good work triangle allows counter space between all three major appliances for facilitating food transfer, preparation and cooking.

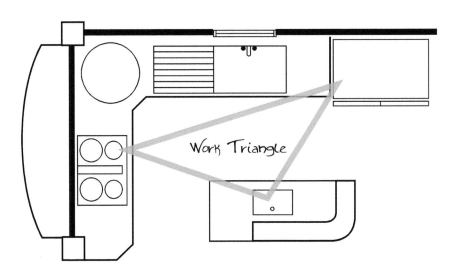

With an island sink two work triangles server this kitchen design.
Design by MCC, Photo page 130

Kitchen Work Triangles

Three major elements: Fire, Water and Metal appear in a standard kitchen. Water appears in the sink and as ice in the refrigerator. Fire appears as the cooktop, stove, toaster oven, hot plate and other heating appliances. Metal appears as the container for both these elements as the stove or refrigerator housing, plus as faucets and appliances. As Fire and Water are opposing elements their placement should be well planned. The sink which is the main Water element should be at the center of the work triangle. Food follows a path from the fridge to the sink for cleaning and prep then to the stove.

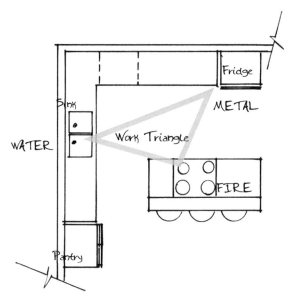

There should be ample countertop between all three. A sink is never located adjacent to the major Fire element, the stove. These two powerful and opposing elements require separation. Designing space between them and using the Wood element neutralizes and balances Fire and Water. Wood can be added by the use of colour and materials.

In many Feng Shui texts the stove cooktop location is an important consideration. It is optimal for the cook to see everything in the kitchen while working. This is for safety and ease of communication with others. Kitchen designs featuring an island with a cooktop is good Feng Shui as it allows for the cook to be social.

In Landscape Feng Shui the idea of good backing in the kitchen is key. When turned away from the kitchen entry or from others in open concept kitchens, an uneasy feeling is created. When the cook is located at an island cooktop, the possibility of a solid wall at their backs is increased. This provides the good backing referred to in Landscape Feng Shui. When the stove and cook face towards a wall the placement of a small mirror on the wall in front of the stove is recommended. A mirror here alerts the cook to anyone arriving in the kitchen or passing behind thus avoiding collisions and surprises. The evolution of modern kitchens are generally in line with good Feng Shui design. Aesthetics and lighting have improved and efficiency increased with better workspaces, appliances and well designed pantry and storage areas. Large does not mean better however. Reevaluating sizes of work triangles for layout and efficiency is especially important in larger kitchen designs.

This kitchen renovation makes use of a limited space with set features such as the sink and fridge. A wall was removed to create an eating area and a work/ play area for children created. Additional storage and a kitchen island includes a stove top. The cook's back is to the dining area, while the cook faces a more open area in the home. The work triangle is kept tight and efficient.

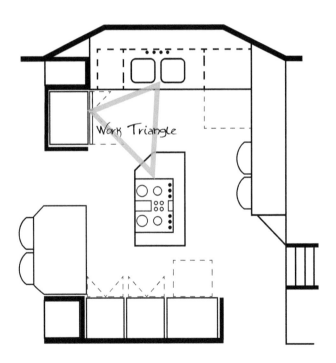

Work Triangle

Many older homes benefit from kitchen makeovers. Even small spaces can make great kitchens when the work triangle and prep issues are addressed.

Apartment Style Kitchens and Work Triangles

Small apartment style kitchens are either efficient or challenging depending on the layout and the efficiency of the work triangle.

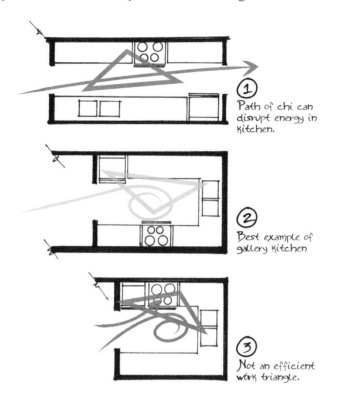

① Path of chi can disrupt energy in kitchen.

② Best example of gallery kitchen

③ Not an efficient work triangle.

The most unfavourable Feng Shui kitchen design is the hallway or galley kitchen which are least likely to allow for pooling chi. They function well used by one occupant. The energy can be disrupted at any time when others walk through. U shaped kitchens afford the most pooling chi.

Illustration 1: This kitchen is well laid out but is the only option for circulation to other parts of the apartment. If there are more than 2 occupants then it can be problematic.

Illustration 2: U shaped kitchens with good work triangles are best. In small spaces this style can function well for multiple cooks.

Illustration 3: An example of a dysfunctional kitchen. This is often the product of a renovation by home owners seeking to add a suite for revenue. Having to move food from a refrigerator to counter space not adjacent or convenient can create stress and mental exhaustion for users. When this layout occurs in a larger space these effects are compounded.

Functional Feng Shui Kitchen Design

The focus in all good Feng Shui design is to meet need with versatility. Spaces should be optimized not wasted. European, especially Scandinavian and Italian design has become trend setting in the West. They feature uncluttered spaces, impressive storage solutions, clean lines and overall efficient use of all space. Small interiors and tiny home designs are economic and ecologically focused bringing back into vogue the idea that less is more. Large kitchens vs. small is a personal aesthetic, yet maintaining good function is key. Individual taste and preference vary from culture to culture. Good Feng Shui design strives for function, practicality and efficiency, without minimizing intimacy.

43)

All the elements are represented in this kitchen. Metal appears in the appliances, sink and grey tones. Fire: in the cook top, and other countertop appliances. Earth appears in the granite countertops and the earth tones. Wood appears in the materials. Water appears in both the sinks and the color black.

DINING AREAS

Separate, overly formal dining rooms, located away from the kitchen are rarely used. Kitchens that provide adequate dining for various occasions render the formal dining room redundant. With consideration for ecology, efficient use of space and more moderate floor plans, dining areas become the new design challenge. Designers and architects now plan tables and seating areas that are expandable, making a dedicated dining room unnecessary. The use of round or oval tables creates pooling chi. Rectangular shaped tables set up a hierarchal energy, with those sitting at the head of the table dominating. This situation results in static chi and diminished energy flow. Round, oval and square shapes equalize the status of those at the table while stimulating more energy flow. Client requirements and budgetary constraints ultimately dictate design. It becomes the responsibility of designers, architects and builders to educate and deliver conscious, creative solutions.

WASHROOMS

Primitive forms of toilets have been around for over 2000 years. Flush toilets and indoor plumbing are relatively new because the idea of disposing human waste so close to sleeping and eating areas was frowned upon. It is essential that washroom placement and layout be carefully considered. In Feng Shui design we recognize the symbolic Yin nature of washrooms. Yin is the dark, hidden, bacterial component of human nature. The goal in Feng Shui design is to minimize this Yin energy from seeping into adjacent spaces so washrooms are typically not located near an entry, a kitchen or a bed. A washroom should never be a focal point at a main entrance. Even at a rear or secondary entrance, mudrooms, laundry rooms and pantries should take precedence. A much overlooked aspect in many washrooms is the sight line to the toilet. In Feng Shui design the overall ambience takes precedence with the focal points being the sink, the cabinetry and other aesthetic components. Toilets as a focal point are simply not attractive.

Designing half walls to separate view lines to the toilets and locating them in their own room is becoming more popular. These design changes allow the washroom experience to be more pleasant for all. Efficient and low budget options can still be aesthetically pleasing.

This older attractive washroom has the ultimate Feng Shui flaw; the toilet is the first item viewed.

Creative design solutions and Feng Shui knowledge are contributing to the washroom evolving into spa-like areas. When a toilet is enclosed or hidden from immediate view, a sanctuary feel is created no matter the bathroom's size. Allowing a healthy separation of these facilities requires intention and creativity.

When applying Feng Shui design note that the SE area of a building is the most unfavourable location for washroom placement. Fortunate Blessings is the universal principle aligned with the SE direction of the Bagua. Water is a prominent element in a washroom. Symbolically it is aligned with life force energy and in Feng Shui this is often associated with money. A toilet in the Fortunate Blessings gua metaphorically flushes wealth away. The SE Direction on the compass may differ if using the 3 Door System. Whatever method used, it is important to note that the SE is associate with the Wood element. A Feng Shui cure in such a washroom is the addition of wood, because water symbolically feeds wood and allows it to grow. Imagery of trees, real plants and the color green can be used to counterbalance the symbology of money being drained.

Washrooms in public Spaces: Many public facilities have a noticeable separation in the form of a double entry or vestibule. This allow access in curvaceous pattern or the Tail of the Dragon.

Created to avoid sight lines, while maintaining security, this transition allows a definite separation between public and private space. Airports and shopping malls are often good examples. Washrooms play an important role in public spaces and as a result better designs are being

44)

Public washroom vestibules can be both practical and fun.

generated. They are, however, rarely made a focal point. Washrooms in front entry halls of public spaces must be given special consideration as to ease of location yet minimal attention.

Restaurant washroom design allows for a variety of experiences. They vary from luxurious to disgusting. How safe we feel eating in the establishment can be a direct reflection of the washroom's design, location and condition.

BEDROOMS

More time is spent in the bedroom than any other space. The immune system regenerates as we sleep, making this space that much more important. Bedrooms have become more active and less restful in recent years. Many things cause disturbances in the bedroom but one of the most prevalent is electromagnetic field radiation. Electronic devices such as flat screen tv's and micro wave energy from cell phones and computers are primary contributors to this phenomena. Bedrooms have become entertainment centers yet its purpose is primarily for sleep and intimacy. Noise and light pollution infuse bedroom areas creating a Yang, active, outgoing quality. This room should be more Yin which is restful, quiet and free of disturbing EMF radiation. Major power sources and main electrical boxes should not be located within a 10 or 12 foot radius of a bed (check upper and lower floors). If living in an apartment one should inquire where these power sources are located. If you notice a shift in sleep patterns in a new space or experience disturbed sleep, check power sources. Recent studies have found power sources to be a contributing factor in leukaemia in young children. Feng Shui practices are simple common sense strategies that improve and create healthy, beneficial and restful sleep.

Avoid bedrooms which are located near

- front doors
- a building's electrical panel
- radiation of any kind (some included in this list)
- microwave towers in the sight line of a bedroom window
- microwave ovens
- mechanical rooms and hot water tanks
- sources of noise pollution
- exterior power lines and transformers
- above garages
- toilets without buffer space such as closets

One overlooked energy activator in bedrooms is a mirror. Mirrors are powerful transmitters of both external and internal electromagnetic energy. One Feng Shui theory is that if you look at a mirror upon waking first thing in the morning you scare your spirit. Taking quiet time in the mornings is good practice when possible. Those who do yoga, meditate or have a practice of inner awareness know the importance of morning energy. There can be is a sudden physical shift from yin to yang as a result of the mirror activation. Feng Shui practitioners advise that mirrors never face you directly across from the bed and that they be minimized in the sleeping area. Covering them is an option. Waking with a sense of disorientation, or being unrested may be a result any number of the disturbances. Quality of sleep and having a healthy immune system is the goal of good Feng Shui design in the bedroom.

A creatively hidden toilet in an Asian bedroom design.

Ideal Feng Shui in the Bedroom

This illustration shows an example of a closet as the buffer space between the bedroom and bathroom. The toilet is at the furthest point from the bed and is set in an area that allows optimal chi flow through the space. The bed is in a quiet zone and the Landscape Feng Shui animals and elements create a balanced secure area for its location. The wall provides good backing as would the proper headboard.

Note that the entry to the bedroom/ ensuite/ dressing area is well placed. Circulation is minimal through the space and the chi can pool in various areas. The room is large enough to provide a private resting, exercise, meditation and sitting area. Although a luxury for some, the privacy of an inner sanctuary is important.

En-suite bathrooms are quite popular in modern design. The question is how close to the sleeping space should they be placed. Bathrooms create an unfavourable Yin energy, believed to be unhealthy for the immune system. Sounds, smells and unpredictable water movement are best located a safe distance from the bed. A buffer zone such as a closet between the bathroom and the sleeping area is good Feng Shui design. Closing doors to en suite areas at night is a good remedial solution as well.

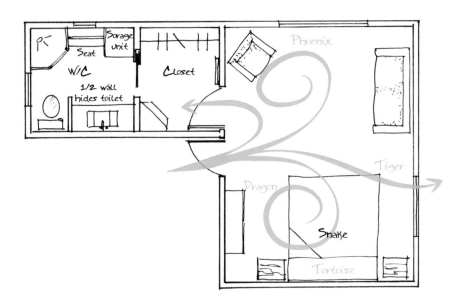

The Dragon is found as a tall storage unit to the left of the head of the bed. There are no windows behind or near the bed. The Tiger is represented by the window to the right which is lower. The Phoenix appears as a window across from the bed. A picture or painting of a landscape could be substituted for a window, allowing a Ming Tang presence. The Snake is at the center of the bed; rested and undisturbed pooling chi. Insomnia can be the result of too many mirrors in a bedroom so they are best placed away from the bed in dressing areas and bathrooms. Minimizing or covering them when sleeping is optimal.

This bedroom has a perfect headboard and good Feng Shui Landscape. The perspective drawing below captures the layout in a smaller version. The solid wall behind the bed acts as the Tortoise. The solid nonmirrored closet doors (unseen in the photo) on the right (left if you are in the bed), acts as the Dragon. The lower windows on the left (to the right if on the bed) opens to a balcony and acts as the Tiger. Across from the bed is a large landscape painting, which acts as the Phoenix. The bed's position allows for pooling chi on the bed and is the Snake position in the room. Chi flows from the door around the space, settles softly on the bed and exits through the balcony doors and windows.

BEDROOM LAYOUT CURES

Bedrooms laid out for optimal health create a pooling chi area around the bed space. When a door aligns directly with a window and the bed is in between, chi does not pool unless curtains or blinds are kept closed. A more yang quality of chi is created; more than should be present when resting. The question is then, how can we invite the 'chi' to stay in the room for awhile before it leaves?

There is also some suspicion that if your feet point out towards the door, it is the corpse position and therefore many Feng Shui specialists advise against it. I agree that it is not the best option. Landscape Feng Shui in the bedroom will often take precedent over directional energy, if the bed is placed in a person's positive direction. In many cases, layouts and chi floe restricted by bedroom size are restricted by bedroom size. In this case, Landscape Feng Shui and how it can be created in a bedroom is a good alternative. Landscape Feng Shui is a good alternative to solve these problems.

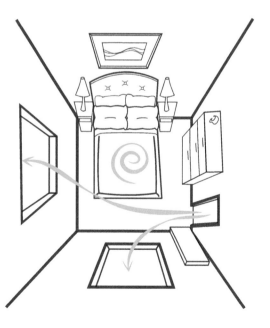

A perspective drawing of the bedroom on page 138, mirrors good Landscape Feng Shui in the photo above. This layout allows optimal Feng Shui in a room. Many bedrooms have limited positions for beds. Checking directional energy of clients or using the Landscape Feng Shui are but guides for health and well being.

Optimal Chi Flow in the Bedroom

BEDROOM A: Unsatisfactory chi flow in a bedroom.

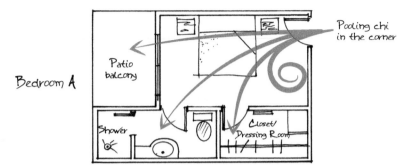

Chi flows directly across the bed so it is not allowed to pool. There is only one small pooling chi area in the sleeping space itself and it is in the corner where a chair could be located. Locating the bed in a pooling chi area is preferred. Chi cutting across the bed to exit at the balcony/ window is disturbing to sleep if the door is left open at night. Chi flows directly into the bathroom and into the dressing room. Depending on the difference in sensitivities of the occupants, this layout may not be a problem. Awareness of these challenges will assist those who are more sensitive.

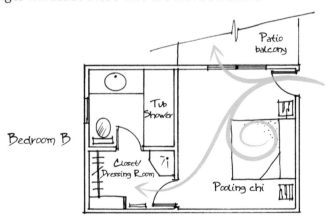

BEDROOM B: Optimal Chi/Energy flow through a bedroom.

Chi flow does not cut across the bed and energy pooling is not interrupted. Chi is directed in a gentler manner. This bedroom has a closet/dressing room buffering the Yin Chi from the sleeping area.

Landscape Feng Shui in the Bedroom

It is possible to micro site Landscape Feng Shui into a bedroom for optimum placement.

Backing~ TORTOISE: Good backing is first and foremost in Landscape Feng Shui and is indicated by the Tortoise location. A solid wall behind the bed is best. Headboards are important as they create additional backing especially if a solid wall is missing in this location. Regardless, strong backing requires a wall or a fabricated wall to protect the physical body when sleeping. Windows at the head of the bed are disruptive so a solid head board at least 18-24 inches high can mitigate disturbances. Chi flowing in from a window can create drafts across the body and is not recommended to come in contact with the head as we sleep. Windows here are best when they are at least 2 feet above the head. Headboards and their shape are also important. Sleigh beds are best as they contain energy and pool chi by the nature of their contained design. Solid head boards incorporating gentle curves are better than slats and irregular designs.

Left Side ~ DRAGON: The left side is the Dragon location and furnishings should be higher here than the right side. This can be a solid wall or a chest of high drawers. Locating a larger lamp on this side of the bed and a lower one on the right to create the balance of Yang Dragon and Yin Tiger is also a solution.

Right Side ~ TIGER: The right side is the Tiger location so physical features on this side should be lower than those on the left. A low set drawers or locating windows on this side is best. Photos can be placed lower on the right wall than the left. Balancing the Yang Dragon and the Yin Tiger requires creativity, imagination and a bit of fun especially when the physical space is challenging.

Front ~ PHOENIX: The Phoenix in front of us while sitting up in a bed should feel open and spacious. Achieved by window placement here, it allows for the concept of Ming Tang. When a window is not possible hanging a painting or print of a fabulous view in this location will create it. This is more important when Ming Tang is not good for the home in general. Rekindling romance can be achieved simply by finding a sensual piece of original art to invoke the Fire element in the Phoenix location. Whether art or a view, what is seen in front should promote a sense of vision and enforce personal space.

Removing televisions from a bedroom promotes good Feng Shui. When a TV is located in the Phoenix/Ming Tang location having a screensaver that reflects a landscape can work. Looking at a blank TV screen negates the Phoenix' purpose.

Center ~ SNAKE: This is located at the center of the bed; an area that should have full command of the space. Pooling Chi and undisturbed energy is required here. Lingering in bed is a luxury and what is felt in this location should be beautiful and inspiring; promoting reflection, rest and inspiration. Dreaming creates both real and symbolic rejuvenation, whether these be sleep or waking dreams. The presence of televisions, computers, or excess mirrors can diminishes this deeper rest. Colors that are restful with added in pillows, art work and fabric create balanced energy. Bedrooms are our sanctuaries, our sacred space and as such should be designed with this in mind.

Landscape Feng Shui can create a sense of balance, ease and relaxation in a bedroom.

Landscape Feng Shui Floor Plan

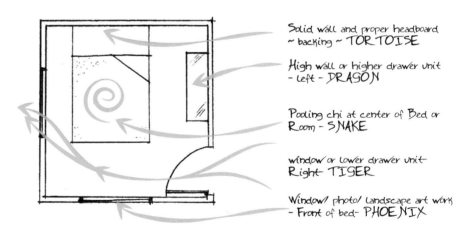

Solid wall and proper headboard ~ backing ~ TORTOISE

High wall or higher drawer unit - Left - DRAGON

Pooling chi at center of Bed or Room - SNAKE

window or lower drawer unit Right TIGER

Window/ photo/ landscape art work - Front of bed - PHOENIX

Note : an expanded perspective of this layout is on page 135

Optimal Headboards

Headboards Matter This illustration shows four different head boards and their symbology. With a variety to choose from use this as a Feng Shui guide.

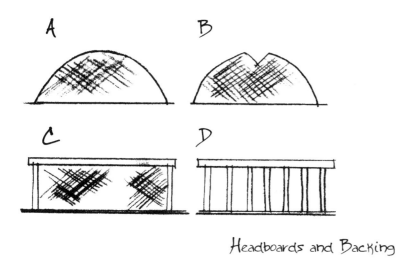

Headboards and Backing

Headboard A The optimal headboard is solid and has a soft gentle curve. It mirrors the natural rise and fall of energy in a day and in life. In Feng Shui it is symbolic of the Tortoise which creates good backing. If it cannot be solid then it should at least look solid. Stiff fabric can be hung behind a bed if a headboard is not available.

Headboard B This headboard has a broken energy via the arrow in the center. This graphic break creates an arrow which is directed at the people in the bed. For a single occupant it is a poison arrow which symbolically attacks. For a couple it creates a split between them and is referred to as a divorce bed.

Headboard C and D A Flat headboard can create flat, non-dynamic and stagnant energy. This energy can affect a marriage. Flat and solid headboards are better than open slatted styles which allow drafts to disturb the head and body while resting.

Good Feng Shui design has to create balance that allows the body relief from tension and stress.

All areas of a bedroom should allow the immune system to benefit from any activity.

RELAXATION SPACES

The areas in which we relax vary from person to person, and from culture to culture. The age of technology has greatly impacted what we refer to as a living room and overall relaxing areas. The living room has evolved from turn of the century show rooms, often reserved for guests only. Now we have a variety of living and resting spaces that are often multifunctional.

In Feng Shui design the focus is on lifestyle and how relaxation affects the body, mind and soul. After the high energy of the day, the body needs to slow down and shift gears. For some, this is more active; for others it is passive. Typically the hours between 3 pm and 9 pm see the energy shift from the active Yang principle to more passive Yin principle. This reflects a progression from awakening to sleeping.

The areas of the home that symbolize the transition from Yang to Yin are the SW, W and NW directions. The sun sets in the west which is a time of relaxation, renewal and enjoyment. In Feng Shui design living and relaxation areas are best located in these directions or guas when possible.

The style and quality of relaxation dictates the space in which it will occur. Prior to the 50's, living rooms were more passive in nature. Since the advent of TV viewing and in the decades since, the quality and variety of resting areas has shifted dramatically. Relaxation areas have become more complex as spaces need to support a multitude of possibilities.

These may include:

- simple living rooms
- relaxation areas near kitchen spaces
- family rooms
- multimedia rooms or home theatres
- formal living or great rooms
- meditation areas
- yoga spaces
- home spas
- exercise and equipment rooms

In essence Feng Shui design has to create a balance especially if active and passive relaxation is required in the same space. The purpose is to allow the body relief and release from tension and stress. All areas of concentration, relaxation and rest should allow the immune system to recharge.

LIVING ROOMS

Living rooms can serve many functions but are primarily for relaxation, gathering, interaction and enjoyment. Located in a variety of places in a home, they are commonly adjacent to a dining or kitchen area. Living and family rooms embody that shift from active yang energy to the quieter more relaxing yin energy symbolized in the Western directions.

The concept of separating space to suit a particular activity is common. Having refuge in our homes after a work day will mean different things to people. Allowing for quiet space to find grounding and peace is more necessary now than ever before. Experiencing rest can be defined by an activity or focal point such as a great view. Understanding the yin/yang principles in designing modern resting areas is a vital part of Feng Shui design. The Yin resting experiences such as sharing, relating, story telling and music playing are being replaced by multi media influences like video gaming which is more Yang. Designating gaming and media viewing areas separate from intimate personal interactions is a way of achieving balance and creating harmony.

Other Combined Spaces

Living rooms are second to the kitchen as main gathering areas. They should be attractive, clean and inviting. All living and resting areas require good seating. Even in small spaces it is imperative to have at least one location to rest in a comfortable chair and be re-energized. Seating areas should not be in circulation spaces or hallways. Placed away from traffic flow they allow pooling chi to be experienced. Seating should be comfortable and plentiful enough for occupants and visitor seating. The concept of creating Pooling Chi areas is crucial for good Feng Shui design.

Great Rooms

Great Rooms, once reserved for stately homes and mansions, have become the norm in large scale residential floor plans. They are generally showpieces that can host events and accommodate various forms of entertainment. Whatever the function they, too, require a balance of Yin and Yang combining the practical with the functional. Great rooms exist outside of day to day relaxation areas. They require extra square footage and can be a drain on resources.

Pooling Chi Areas

All areas of the home require Pooling Chi areas especially in relaxation areas. Well designed circulation space does not interfere with the potential for such areas. Pooling chi spots can be small and simple such as a comfortable arm chair off in a corner with good lighting. It can also be an elaborate living room seating area that invites gathering, sharing and relaxation.

This open floor plan is defined by the furniture arrangement which by the shape, materials and colour attracts attention. The curves and round table invite chi to pool and restricts movement through the space.

MULTI USE RELAXATION AREAS

Multiple use areas are more common in today's designs. They include:

- a bedroom that doubles as a yoga space
- kitchen, eating and relaxation rooms
- living rooms as multi media areas
- workstations in living spaces

The importance in Feng Shui Design is balance. Activities that bring strong Yang active energy to areas that are designed for resting defeat the purpose. Locating computer stations in bedrooms and or gaming consoles in quiet rest areas are examples. Other factors that create disturbances in relaxing areas are:

- sound pollution
- bright lighting
- exterior lighting
- bathroom adjacency without thought to sight lines

Creating new ways to fully relax in homes and buildings is a reflection of our expanded world view. Spas, exercise rooms, yoga spaces, theatre and viewing rooms support specific functions. Awareness of the quality of Chi needed for each space and how to achieve it is a challenge for design professions.

Collecting information about what is required by a client is called a Program for Design. This detailed investigation should determine all the client needs and wants for a design whether it be a new build or a renovation. Design professionals can include or suggest multi-use areas in locations that are obvious. Well thought out rest areas at both work and in the home are becoming more crucial to health and well being in our fast paced lives.

FENG SHUI HOUSE DESIGN

Careful consideration was give to the placement and layout of each room in this Feng Shui Home design.

Upper floors

Things to note:

- the path of chi through the home and entry shows how it greets, from the immediate arrival to the views to a feature wall, allowing one to arrive

- the slow reveal of the interior spaces

- fire place, stairs and washroom placement away from the center of the home

- pooling chi areas that are away from general circulation space

- pass through from the mud room into the kitchen

- the open space and high ceiling in living room expands the space

- the library den open to the space and view

- the master bedroom's separation from the washroom

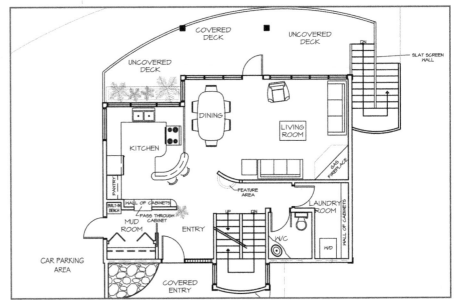

First floor

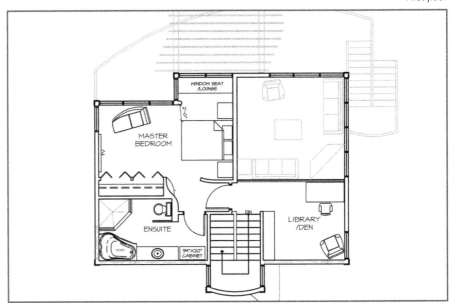

Second floor

Elemental Feng Shui ~ The Art of Orientation

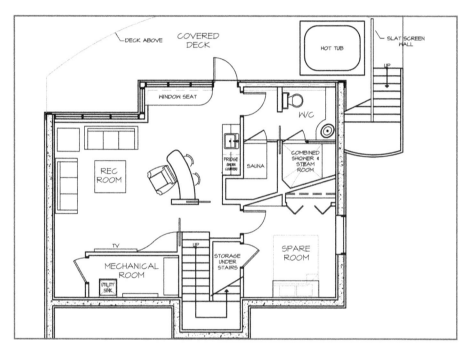

Third floor

Lower floor

- Space doubles as a TV room and entertainment space complete with wet bar and lots of seating options

- spare room is removed and in a quiet area

- the external hot tub is adjacent to interior spa space

PROGRAMS FOR DESIGN: Use and Value

A Program for Design is the information gathered for new design and development projects. Its purpose is to create clarity and specify design requirements. Information gathered reflects the function and needs of a client or client group and allows for evaluation of a project prior to the actual design phase. It allows for clients to voice their wish list then match that to a budget. The design vision is then sculpted into real and attainable objectives. Predesign and a program allows the vision, which starts with the ideas, that translate into a plan. Spaces are defined by bubbles (called bubble diagrams) which are drawn in circles adjacent to each other; functions and areas written in each one. Individual spaces in these bubble diagrams are then assigned square footages. This stage of the process eventually becomes the bones of a good design. Whether it be land, commercial or residential design, this process takes us from the dream to the reality. Budget and scale of a project guides the design process. A good program allows the design phase to go faster. It enables changes and modifications prior to the construction of a project. Programs for Design encourage changes in the pre building stage that can keep costs down and budgets reasonable. The cost of making changes during the building phase can skyrocket quickly. My first position in the design world as a Facilities Programmer was eye opening. Crafting a design by words for client departments, then handing it over to the designers with out being able to design it myself, was frustrating. Over time I realized how important this phase was for good design development. This process serves design professionals, allowing them to create cost efficient, functional, efficient and aesthetic spaces.

ECOLOGY IN DESIGN

Ecology and sustainable design is now taking hold in many fields of design and development. Material costs and availability along with improved construction methods have people seeking alternative solutions. Climate change is becoming a real life constraint. Trends are reflecting smaller building footprints and new innovative technologies. The use of shipping containers, bermed earth homes and the utilization of narrow spaces between existing buildings in large cities are now smart solutions to affordable housing. Innovations in this field are turning heads for young and old who cannot afford to mortgage their future away, yet want quality and earth friendly homes. Changing professional attitudes is a challenge but in Feng Shui Design practical, aesthetic, human and earth friendly designs are the goal. A phrase that impacted me early on was a quote that described Feng Shui as 'the original environmental impact statement'. It provoked and inspired me over the years. As an art, Feng Shui allows conscious consideration of all aspects of human existence. Feng Shui Design allows for us to cut down on waste and consumption while creating healthy, energized buildings.

CONCLUSION:

Feng Shui is a 5000 year old form of placement and orientation developed in the ancient cultures of China, Northern India and Tibet. It revealed to them a core relationship between natural phenomena and cycles of time. Although wind and water exists in each of us, the understanding of Feng Shui is shrouded in mystery and confusion. With the elements at its base, we see their relationship to physical form and how they influence our placement within the environment. By understanding these relationships we actively investigate all expressions of reality.

Feng Shui invites us to look beyond ourselves and recognize the basic human truths found on the Bagua compass. Representing vision, relationship, creativity, benefactors, livelihood, knowledge, community and abundance, these universal concepts allow us to discover more about who we are. In exploring our relationship to the planet in a conscious way, through who we are elementally and in design, we can create great spaces in which to live and work. This book is a western perspective with a view to a deeper understanding of our human imprint on the world.

Gallery

FENG SHUI MIRRORED IN OTHER CULTURES

46) Painted by Wayan Karja, a Balinese artist, who, with reverent understanding of his culture, delves deep into its soul for inspiration. This painting oddly mirrors many aspects of Feng Shui, such as the Bagua Compass and the Magic Square of the Nine Star Ki System. What looks like a simple painting holds a multi layered infusion of Indian, Chinese and Indonesian influences and a myriad of information via the colors, their positions and their relevance to time, place and the human experience.

Cultural embellishment for special occasions heightens the energy of this already magnificent entranceway.

City scape captures all the elements; can you pick them out?

Bali Feng Shui: Water, Wood and the Fire of sunrise.

47) In a home we would consider this protruding office boardroom as escaping energy. The nature of business is Yang and draws from the environment. What do you think?

An apartment building offers a great interior shapes and balcony ratio. Prominent elements are Water and Earth.

48) Before

48) After

Rural Feng Shui

49)

Before

49)

Creating inner sanctuaries

49)

After

After the Feng Shui consultation the client used his unique wood design to define the inner sanctuary from the parking lot area. In doing so it created not more intimate space but it embellished the home's overall look. Located across from a T-junction, the home needed a similar barrier application at the road. This was created with a berm and a wood structure that was a continuation of the same artistic theme. The overall effect allowed definition from public space and his workshop in the parking lot from the home space. The entry into the back area of the yard is now mysterious and private.

Urban Law Office

A new urban law office located in a Historical building with limited natural light. This long space was perfect for a Feng Shui Design solution. For the Chi to flow easily and softly the layout had to take a serpentine route. Adding the Water element to balance the client's elemental chart was a primary consideration. A curved window wall added the shape of water while allowing more light to penetrate the space. The color blue was added in accents and was complimentary to the natural brick wall which was left as feature in his office. A curved reception area also softens the long shape of the room and creates movement through the space.

The curves and color blue are to bring in a much needed Water element to the space.

The only natural light sources are the office window and door into the inner area that has no windows and gives the primary area of the business full view of the outer office with a sense of privacy as well. The table shape also allows a sense of freedom and simplicity. The Mirror provides direction of energy flow within the long narrow space and creates a more serpentine pathway.

Mirror diverts chi in the long narrow space.

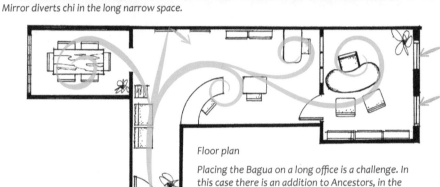

Floor plan

Placing the Bagua on a long office is a challenge. In this case there is an addition to Ancestors, in the entrance and Vision/ Fame and in the boardroom.

50)

50)

50)

Lighting was an important consideration as the only natural light came from the front office which faces north. The use of glass block in the boardroom gives the space access to an adjacent office with natural lighting from the South. Feature lighting by means of a favored chandelier, overhead pot lights and track lighting for art gives the space warmth, personality and versatility.

ACKNOWLEDGEMENTS

I want to acknowledge First Nations wisdom and those who inspire a natural way of being with and taking care of mother earth. With great respect I want to thank my teachers Susan Powell and Roy Parcels. Their wisdom taught me about co-creating with her beauty.

I want to thank my strong mother Florence and my father Moe, whose adventuring spirit and wanderlust was key to my fascination with other cultures. Thank you to my sister Maureen who encouraged me in tough times and for support during this process. I want to thank her four fierce and powerful daughters who also succumbed to mine and Moe's wanderlust. Deep gratitude for my children Tristan and Esperanza and their father Pietro who have witnessed my growth, and transformation. Strong family backing and support is a powerful Feng Shui teaching.

I want to thank the many teachers who influenced me. Their idealism inspired me to be a better person, to ask questions and to always follow my dreams. Thank you to Marion Peters, my first Feng Shui teacher and Roberts Sachs my Nine Star Ki guru.

I acknowledge grandmaster Feng Shui Practitioner Dr. Jes Lim of Qi Mag International. Master Lim is a living example of transforming energy at all levels for human and spacial healing. Also a special thanks to Eric Dowset my dowsing master. His inspired philosophy teaches the power of letting go of drama in order to be clear. Their teachings, wisdom and depth of knowledge lives in my work.

I want to acknowledge Celesttina Hart, Della Burford and Norah Burford for their inspiration and mentorship. I also want to acknowledge the backing of Ladies of the Lake, a powerful group of Kootenay women who understand the importance and ever growing politics of Wind and Water.

I want to thank Tim Turner Davis, Yvonne Nowakowski, and Emil Patenaude. A very special to thanks Brian Peterson and Maureen Kokoska, as my main editors, Brian for his brutal attention to detail and Maureen for her eagle eye. A huge thanks to Peeriya Tiparos whose graphic design has make this book truly Feng Shui.

Finally big gratitude for my dear friends and communities that formed and nourished me over the years. A warm thank you to my Qi Mag associates, colleagues and clients worldwide. And finally to my Canadian Cultural Heroes, David Susuki and Wade Davis whose lives and work have inspired me for many years. Special thank you Wade Davis for the encouragement to just get this information out there!

Blessings to all and especially to those friends and supporters who are not mentioned but are close to my heart. Thank You.

PHOTO CREDITS & ADDITIONAL INFORMATION

All photos and illustrations not credited below are by the author. Book layout; collaboration between author and Peeriya Tiparos-Corfield.

1) Dan Irvine of Stonegarden Studio, Vernon BC. Photo taken by Dan Irvine

2) Pietro Comelli finishes a yurt he assembled/built for Nelson, BC, Canada

3) Hearther Martin-Mcnab, Woven basket artistry. Salt Spring Island BC, Canada

4) Anthropology Museum at UBC, Vancouer BC, Canada

5) Georgetown, Penang, Malaysia. UNESCO World Heritage Site since 2008.

6) Besakih Temple, Karangasem, Bali, Indonesia.

7) 'Water House', Design colaberation by Gabrille Sinclair, Mike Finley and Cam Kuch, Nelson, BC, Canada

8) Gili Air Island, Gili Indah, North Lombok Regency, West Nusa Tennggara, Indonesia

9) Langkawi Island, Langkawi Permata Kedah Archipelago, Malaysia

10) Yin Yang symbol. A personalized design by author

11) Kunjapuri Devi Mandir Temple, near Rishikesh, Uttarakhand, India

12) Feng Shiu design by author for the Costa Rica Yoga Spa, Norasra, Costa Rica, CA

13) Photo courtasy of Peggy De Vries, Certified Financial Planner, Nelson, BC, Canada

14) Dragon energy at The Mother Temple, Besakih, below Sacred Mount Agung, Bali, Indonesia

15) Looking south from Tipi Camp, Pilot Point, Kootenay Lake, BC, Canada

16) Big Rock, Okatoks, Alberta, Canada

17) Photo taken by Bill Weaver, Hagia Sofia Cathedral, Istanbul, Turkey

18) Feng Shui renovation, Photo compliments of P. Yakura, Vancouver, BC Canada

19) Swans Brewery, Pub and Hotel, Victoria, BC, Canada

20) Naritasan Shinshoji Fire Temple, Narita, Japan

21) Halifax Central Library, Halifax, NS, Canada

22) Chaco Culture National Historical Park, UNESCO World Heritage Center, NM, USA

23) Photo courtesy of Qi-Mag International Feng Shui & Geobiology Institute and Dr. Jes Lim

24) Typical Adobe Architecture found in Santa Fe, NM, USA

25) The Galeria Trees Sculpture, Calgary, AB, Canada

26) Hotel walkway, Tokoyo, Japan

27) Office tower refelcting gold, Calgary, AB Canada

28) Water fall photo courtesy of Tristan and Pietro Comelli, South Korea

29) Typical entrance over water in Pennestanen, Bali, Indonesia

30) Stained Glass Art and Photo by Maasa Craig, Nelson, BC

31) Apartment buildings in Penang, Malasyia

32) Sharma Springs; tallest bamboo structure in the Green Village, Badung, Bali, Indonesia

33) Green Village Houses, Badung, Bali, Indonesia

34) Kovalum Lighthouse, Kovalum, Kerala, India

35) Photo taken by Jasmine Crystal Jones, Kuala Lampur, Malaysia

36) A Typical 'Meru Tower', shaped to honor the Hindu god Meru, Bali, Indonesia

37) Open walled washroom with mirrors in a bamboo home. Green Village, Badung, Bali, Indonesia

38) Traditional roof shapes, Campuhan Ridge walk, Ubud, Bali, Indonesia

39) A local landmark, Arbutus Cafe, Vancouver, BC Canada

40) Basement apartment Feng Shui adjustment. Photo Compliments of Monica Kendel, Victoira, BC, Canada

41) Photo compliements of Lana and Dave Asprey, prior to Feng Shui adjustment, Cobble Hill, BC, Canada

42) Marina's Hidaway B&B. Design and photo compliments of Georgene Brunell, Gabriolla Island, BC, Canada

43) FS Kitchen design, Water House * See # 7, photo compliemts Stacey and Mike Finley, Nelson, BC, Canada

44) Whimsical WC vestibule, River Market, New Westminister, BC, Canada

45) Marina's Hidaway B&B, Photos compliments of Georgene Brunell, Gabriolla Island, BC, Canada

46) Image by Wayan Karja, Son of a member of 'The Young Artists of the 1970's', Pennestanen, Bali, Indonesia

47) Telus Gardens, Vancouver, BC, Canada

48) Collaborative Feng Shui Design for P. Yakura, * see # 18, Vancouver, BC, Canada

49) Colaborative Feng Shui Solutuon, Photos compliments Heibert (Harry) Heisinger, Cobble Hill, BC, Canada

50) Feng Shui Design for Pigott and Co., Photos compliments Pigott Law Office, Nelson, BC Canada

Illustrations pages 114, 145; Feng Shui design by author in colaboration with and for P. Yakura, Vancouver, BC. Architecture, Structural & Drawings by Robert Mattias, Mattias Architects, Trail, BC

INDEX

ABOUT THE AUTHOR

Photo by Fabrizio
Belardetti Photgraphy

www. adarsashuideva.com
shuideva@gmail.com
Charlyne
250 509 0536

M. Charlyne Chiasson is an Interior Designer, Feng Shui Consultant, Geomancer, Nine Star Ki Astrologer and Writer who travels extensively. Born and raised on Cape Breton Island, Nova Scotia, Charlyne won a scholarship to study Clothing and Textiles at Mount St. Vincent University in Halifax but switched her focus to Interior Design after only one year at the Mount. She then did a semester of Fine Arts at Morningside College in Sioux City, Iowa to create a portfolio to gain entry into the Interior Design program at Ryerson University in Toronto. After a 5 month solo trip to Europe, Northern Africa and the British Isles she commenced her studies and received an Interior Design Degree from Ryerson in 5 years. Charlyne took a full year off in the middle the 4 year program to work

full time in Yellowknife, NWT, where she had gone for a summer job after her first year at Ryerson. She returned to Yellowknife after obtaining her degree to accept a position as a Facility Programmer for the North West Territorial Government. This position required travel and over the years she witnessed cultural shifts in government with the inception of Nunavut and independent self rule in the north. Her time in the Arctic impacted her design career. Upon leaving the north, Charlyne traveled to Latin America for 14 months and then to Asia frequently, while also working part time in the silviculture industry in BC. In 1990 she and her partner decided to live full time in Nelson, BC to raise their young family. Charlyne started her Feng Shui studies in 1993, first independently then with

several teachers. She started her Feng Shui design business in 1997. In 2003 Charlyne earned a Feng Shui Diploma from Qi-Mag International, a school started in Sri Lanka by the Asian Grandmaster Dr. Jes Lim. Her studies with Qi-Mag have taken her across North America, Mexico, Spain and Austria to upgrade and add to her Feng Shui knowledge. Charlyne also studied with Eric Dowsett, a personal and environmental dowsing professional over several years. His teachings have been an integral part of her Feng Shui career over the last 15 years. Charlyne travels to work, teach and write and has written many articles for various publications. This is Charlyne's first book on Feng Shui Design.

 FriesenPress

Suite 300 - 990 Fort St
Victoria, BC, V8V 3K2
Canada

www.friesenpress.com

ISBN
978-1-5255-1096-0 (Hardcover)
978-1-5255-1097-7 (Paperback)
978-1-5255-1098-4 (eBook)

1. ARCHITECTURE, INTERIOR DESIGN, FENG SHUI

2. ENVIRONMENTAL STUDIES

Distributed to the trade by The Ingram Book Company

CPSIA information can be obtained
at www.ICGtesting.com
Printed in the USA
LVHW07*2310170918
590467LV00002B/2/P

9 781525 510960